Aurelia, Aurélia

Also by Kathryn Davis

The Silk Road
Duplex
The Thin Place
Versailles
The Walking Tour
Hell
The Girl Who Trod on a Loaf
Labrador

Aurelia, Aurélia

A Memoir

Kathryn Davis

Graywolf Press

Excerpt from *The Tibetan Book of the Dead: First Complete Translation* edited by Graham Coleman with Thupten Jinpa, translated by Gyurme Dorje, translation copyright © 2005 by The Orient Foundation (UK) and Gyurme Dorje. Used by permission of Viking Books, an imprint of Penguin Publishing Group, a division of Penguin Random House LLC. All rights reserved.

This publication is made possible, in part, by the voters of Minnesota through a Minnesota State Arts Board Operating Support grant, thanks to a legislative appropriation from the arts and cultural heritage fund. Significant support has also been provided by Target Foundation, the McKnight Foundation, the Lannan Foundation, the Amazon Literary Partnership, and other generous contributions from foundations, corporations, and individuals. To these organizations and individuals we offer our heartfelt thanks.

MINNESOTA
STATE ARTS BOARD

CLEAN
WATER
LAND &
LEGACY
AMENDMENT

Published by Graywolf Press
250 Third Avenue North, Suite 600
Minneapolis, Minnesota 55401

www.graywolfpress.org

Published in the United States of America

ISBN 978-1-64445-078-9

2 4 6 8 9 7 5 3 1
First Graywolf Printing, 2022

Library of Congress Control Number: 2021940575

Cover design: Jeenee Lee

Cover art: Anne Davis, *Kate's Dog*

For Louise

There is no other way to understand the procession of dachshunds that follows Kathryn's disastrous recital than as a looking glass into Kathryn's tempestuous soul. If we were to translate her soul into words, it would say: "Look at me! No! Don't look at me! Look at those dogs instead!"

Miguel Morales

As everybody knows, one never sees the sun in one's dreams.

Gérard de Nerval

Aurelia, Aurélia

Time Passes

There are points in your life when you think you're about to become whatever's next. I was sixteen; I had read the entire *Alexandria Quartet* and I thought I was an adult. I had read sentences like "Watching her thus, trapped for a moment by a rare sunbeam on the dirty window-pane, I could not help reflecting once more that in her there was nothing to control or modify the intuition which she had developed out of a nature gorged upon introspection" and had understood nothing except the stupendous effect the language had on me. "Empty cadences of sea-water licking its own wounds, sulking along the mouths of the delta, boiling upon those deserted beaches . . ."

The first time I inhabited Alexandria it was as a sixteen-year-old high school student living in Philadelphia, the second time, as a twenty-three-year-old married woman living on a Greek island. I was trying to teach myself demotic Greek, using a pocket dictionary and a beautiful two-volume edition of the poetry of C. P. Cavafy. The second time I felt like anything but an adult, a girl in old woman's clothing, an impostor, climbing up and down the steep paths of the island every morning with the real old women, all of us dressed in black, all of us looking for kindling. The fallen wood was slick and wet; it was the worst winter anyone could remember. My husband—the first one—was very sick, the *kalýva* we were renting was cold and damp, and the only thing I could find to start a fire were old *Playboy* magazines, the paper also slick and wet. I hated my husband. I hated being married. We hated each other, the idea having been that coming to Skiathos would save us from our misery.

"You will find no new lands, you will find no other seas . . ." So Cavafy wrote of Alexandria in "The City." Book in hand I looked back at myself, book in hand. In between came the part of my life called "Time Passes."

The first section of *To the Lighthouse* occupies only a single day, all of it spent delving into the psyche of each of the central characters, rolling them into a great, teeming ball of psyches like the shawl around the skull of the beast in the nursery bedroom. Its governing question is deceptively simple: Will it be possible to make a trip to the lighthouse tomorrow? Mrs. Ramsay says, "Yes, of course, if it's fine," and her son James is filled with "an extraordinary joy" until his father shows up. "It won't be fine," Mr. Ramsay says, looking out the window. The day could be fine; the day could be not fine. The day could be both things at once.

When I was a girl of sixteen in Philadelphia who thought she was an adult, my first encounter with Virginia Woolf was like that day, fine and not fine. The only thing I knew about her came from the title of Edward Albee's play, which some of us had considered putting on until we were told it wouldn't be appropriate. When I asked my English teacher what the title meant, he handed me a copy of *To the Lighthouse*. "You'll like this," he said. "It's difficult. She writes about difficult human relationships." Following the bilious confusion of Durrell, Virginia Woolf's language—which despite the complexity of her sensibility is remarkably clean and clear—entered my soul (to steal her imagery) like a beak.

I didn't need a dictionary to read this book, nor did it drive me to the thesaurus. I didn't need to have experienced true love or sex or marriage or parenthood or old age or death—subjects I continued to write about, energetically, cluelessly—to make a powerful connection with it. I think this was possible because, despite the book's interest in these matters, the dark drumming heart of it, the place I remember best from when I first read it and the place I still return to with quickening breath, is the shortest and weirdest section, the section that announces itself to be, by virtue of its title and everything in it, pure transition.

I was an adult. I'd read *The Alexandria Quartet*. I'd gone to Europe on a student ship (the *Aurelia*—the student ship everyone seems to have crossed the Atlantic on in the sixties) where each evening they showed a foreign film in the auditorium. I sat with a group of college students. I wore a paisley scarf, peasant-style and, briefly, feigned a Russian accent. The great mystery of *The Seventh Seal* was compounded of the film itself (unlike any movie I had seen in my life) and the fact that I couldn't understand what anyone was saying until I read the subtitles. There were Swedish words that thrilled me to the bone. *Skat. Riddare. Döden.* It was like the word *rook* in *To the Lighthouse*. Sound overpowered meaning, as if the word had come into existence first, the thing it defined after.

You could try on personae like dresses. I didn't just want to write like Virginia Woolf; I wanted to *be* Virginia Woolf. I wanted the brilliant, dogmatic father; the soulful, extroverted mother. I wanted the house on a Hebridean island. I wanted the eyelids. "Heart's dearest, why do you cry?" the old German professor asked rebellious Jo March, and so I married my first husband because he was German and ten years older than me. There he was, theatrically coughing and gasping for breath on a narrow, damp mattress in a Greek *kalýva* , as meanwhile I fed olive branch after olive branch into the woodstove. My husband was dying of typhoid on the floor of a one-room hospital, the sirocco flinging sand at the windowpane. I was Paul Bowles; I was writing "the whole monstrous star-filled sky turning sideways before her eyes."

We came to Skiathos so my husband could scout locations for a movie based on *The Murderess*, a book about an old woman named Hadoula who throws girl babies down a well to spare them sorrow later. He had in mind an actress, a rich woman who had taken his film classes, to play the part of Hadoula. We had no money—we were living on yogurt. When you're young, the economic picture is hazy if not invisible, the word *economic* like gas, like smoke, like the sublimating force of my husband's illness. We both knew he wasn't dying, but something was dying, something more like our original fantasy. To get to the north shore I had to climb over the island's central spine, a steep mountain crisscrossed by paths made by goats. Olive trees gave way to fig trees, their branches pruned to look like fists. At some point there was a monastery you weren't supposed to enter if you were a woman but I went in anyway. For a while I was nowhere, chill enfolding me like a cloak.

"I wish sometimes to be less an imagination and more a person," I wrote. I didn't know where or what I was, really. I lived in a body but there was part of me that seemed, like Virginia Woolf, capable of functioning without one.

The opening section isn't the best part of *To the Lighthouse*, nor is "The Lighthouse," the third and final section. Will they make a trip to the lighthouse? Yes, they will. Do they make a trip to the lighthouse? Yes, they do. To get to write "Time Passes," Virginia Woolf had to write those other two sections; there's no such thing as transition without there being a point of departure or a point of arrival. We need to know something about the Ramsays' marriage, about their children, Lily's painting, Mr. Ramsay's boots. The rooks. The skull on the nursery wall. We need to know something about what it is we're being asked—have been asked, will be asked—to pay attention to, as it's in the process of becoming whatever is next.

"Time Passes" begins with a series of disembodied utterances, pronouncements really, almost as if the speakers are speaking to themselves.

Well, we must wait for the future to show.
It's almost too dark to see.
One can hardly tell which is the sea and which is the land.
Do we leave that light burning?
No. Not if everyone's in.

One minute you're in the drawing room with Mr. and Mrs. Ramsay, the next minute you don't know where you are. One minute you're a girl who thinks she's an adult. The next thing you know, you're on the threshold of a world that seems impossible to enter, even though you have no alternative. You're in the dark, hearing voices. "So with the lamps all put out, the moon sunk, and a thin rain drumming on the roof a downpouring of immense darkness began. Nothing, it seemed, could survive the flood, the profusion of darkness which, creeping in at keyholes and crevices, stole round window blinds, came into bedrooms, swallowed up here a jug and basin . . ."

The shawl around the skull on the nursery wall is coming undone. Everything of vital importance having to do with human beings is happening here, swiftly, in brackets. Prue Ramsay gets married. Prue Ramsay dies in childbirth, Andrew Ramsay gets killed by an exploding shell in France.

"[Mr. Ramsay, stumbling along a passage one dark morning, stretched his arms out, but Mrs. Ramsay having died rather suddenly the night before, his arms, though stretched out, remained empty.]"

This place is like no house we've ever lived in. The rules governing this place are as real as those that pertain on the astral plane; it's like no house we've ever known—there are *all* new lands here, *all* new seas. We're in the place of transition, the point of intersection between the rook in Virginia's brain and the rook in ours, a place of communion between psyches, the skull laid bare, the place of breath, the expulsion of souls, a space or time as vast and long or small and brief as our experience of space/time itself.

Lost

There is the moment you step off the edge of the cliff before you hit the ground. The moment you open the door before you step inside. This moment can last a second or it can last a lifetime. "They heard the two horses munching leaves." A paragraph that is a single sentence swells to occupy all the space between the moment Rodolphe puts his arm around Emma Bovary's waist and the moment he leads her deeper into the woods. Between "And I will show you something different from either / Your shadow at morning striding behind you / Or your shadow at evening rising to meet you; / I will show you fear in a handful of dust" and "Don't tell me what I can't do."

The experience of leaping into space is a thrilling one. You leave the page behind and if you're lucky you're granted access to the mind of the person who wrote what was on it. Certain art forms—literature, music, film, the ones that exist in time or take time for their subject—lend themselves to this experience. Jean Seberg in a convertible without a mirror, Jean Seberg in a convertible with a mirror. An ape throws a bone in the air, a space satellite rotates back. The wild leap Beethoven makes from sweetness to discord at the end of Opus 134. And there you are, ghostly you and the ghostly artist, in ghostly communion in that nonexistent place between words, images, notes.

A Buddhist calls this period of transition a lifetime, the great transition between birth and death.

I came late to *Lost*. The show first aired on September 22, 2004; I didn't start watching until the spring of 2009. I'd been told I would love the show by people who knew me well enough to know my preference for the enigmatic. Sometimes, before I began to watch, I would overhear conversations about *Lost* and I remember experiencing a feeling of curiosity akin to longing. I was told *The Third Policeman* makes an appearance during the second season. I was told Eternity did too.

Time passed and, as so often happens under these circumstances, things changed. My husband—not the husband of the Greek island—was diagnosed with an aggressive form of cancer and had to undergo surgery. There were post-surgical complications; it was obvious we needed something to distract us from everything else that was going on. In other words, we needed something to watch. By this point the first three seasons of *Lost* were available on DVD. It didn't show up on Netflix until much later.

Even if you've never seen the show you probably know the premise: It starts with a scene of catastrophe, the wreckage of a large airplane—Oceanic Flight 815—on a beach. People are wailing, pieces of fuselage are in flame, a man gets sucked into a still-whining jet engine. It's unclear where this is, exactly, and it's unclear what brought the plane down, though while a plane crash is not an everyday occurrence, there is nothing especially *otherworldly* about such a thing. It's only gradually that we begin to see that the place where these people find themselves isn't the predictable tropical island paradise it first looks like. Beating through jungle underbrush they come upon a polar bear; an animate cloud of smoke that is really a monster pours forth from a bamboo forest. There is unearthly howling. There is a hatch leading who knows where.

What I found most compelling about *Lost* is the same thing that came to turn off many of its viewers, even its so-called die-hard fans. After a while the delectable inexplicability of everything about the island, starting with the polar bear and the smoke monster and continuing through weeks of characters disappearing without a trace (young Walt), characters appearing as if from out of thin air (Daniel Faraday), characters miraculously cured (John Locke), characters dying and reappearing (Boone Carlyle), the popping up of clues (*The Third Policeman!*), the popping up of clues that ultimately led nowhere (characters named Locke and Faraday and Carlyle and Rousseau and Hume), of mysterious recurrence (the numbers 4 8 15 16 23 42 showing up as the serial number for the hatch and Hurley's winning lottery number, as well as being the numbers that won the Mega Millions lottery for 41,763 *Lost* fans and the coefficients in an equation that predicts the end of life as we know it), and, finally, of the growing suspicion that the creators of the series (Damon Lindelof, Carlton Cuse, Jeffrey Lieber, and J. J. Abrams) never had an explanation in mind for why and how a particular group of people managed to survive a plane crash that was impossible to survive (in which the entire tail section of an aircraft broke off midair)—after a while all of this delectable inexplicability began to drive people, and not just denizens of the island, crazy.

A series like *Lost*—any television series meant to be watched over a period of time—involves built-in, inevitable moments of transition, moments that can last as long as or longer than a week between episodes, or as brief as the instant it takes a binge watcher to switch from one episode to the next. During these moments you think you're leaving behind the tropical island you've gotten lost on and re-entering whatever constitutes "real life," the interminable dark and seesawing ramp of the hospital parking garage, for instance, or the cramped room in which you sit surrounded by the bright young faces of your husband's medical team. The only difference is that the parking garage and consultation room have now become liminal space, places of transition where time behaves differently, where the ending—if even a thing like an ending exists—is unknown, where neither the number stamped on your parking garage ticket nor your husband's PSA number will come to mean what you think they do.

The thing about cancer—about any human malady that doesn't have a knowable cause (not like bubonic plague, say, or rabies)—is that it seems bestowed haphazardly, the system governing its bestowal as inscrutable as the system prevailing on the island. Routinely you feel like some rational explanation is approaching from very far off, on the horizon, something you might end up being able to see, like the freighter *Kahana*, something that appears to be coming to save you but turns out to be bent on doing the exact opposite and has to be blown up. All appears to be lost— *Lost!*—and then someone in a mysterious station that has only recently made an appearance on the island turns a giant wheel.

Think of the island as a record spinning on a turntable, we're told, only now, that record is skipping. Whatever happened down at the Orchid station . . . I think . . . it may have . . . dislodged us. Dislodged us from what? someone asks. From time, we're told.

Thin air, nowhere, without a trace, impossible to survive—all of these are key words and phrases, as is the end of life as we know it. From "time present and time past" to "time past and time future." From "two horses munching leaves" to "go go go, said the bird: human kind cannot bear very much reality."

Crush

We're in a room on the ground floor of a hotel, the bed facing a wall of curtained windows that in turn faces the street. It is nighttime; rain is coming down, steadily, reflectively, a steady stream of passersby visible through the curtains, which are sheer. Everyone is moving in the same direction, bent slightly forward and holding an umbrella, from left to right, the good direction, from past to future, the opposite of where Death leads the knight and the squire and the monk and the smith and the mute in their final dance against the backdrop of time in *The Seventh Seal.* The umbrella is the canopy of the heavens; the rain is never going to let up. We can see the passersby but they can't see us, though Eric has turned on a light above his side of the bed.

I was obsessed with *The Seventh Seal* my senior year in high school; I was obsessed with the vision it presented of a handsome knight playing a game of chess with Death. Death's face was unexpectedly round and blindingly white, the blackness of his eyes and their sparkling avidity as terrifying as the sound of his name in Swedish. *Döden.* There could be no doubt of the fact that death at the end of it elevated life—an otherwise lackluster affair in which human beings were obliged to eat and mate and have jobs and engage in pointless conversation—into a realm worthy of passionate attachment. The knight was handsome, yes, and virtuous (though not a very good chess player, according to my best friend Peggy's older brother Marto), but Death was overfull of something that seemed more like life than whatever it was that animated the knight. When the knight said, "You drew black," Death replied, "Appropriate, don't you think?" Unlike everyone else in the movie, he had a sense of humor. I was in love with Death. If I couldn't have him, I would settle for someone like Marto, a handsome, quick-witted ne'er-do-well.

In the dream, Eric is propped against the pillows, restless, paging through a newspaper, scattering and discarding pages across the bedspread, which is heavily quilted in hues of old gold and dusty rose. Normally I would have removed such a bedspread and jammed it into the closet. "I've had it," Eric says. I remind him that first we have to meet family. We can fake it, he says. He's been ready to leave for a long time. "I thought we were happy," I say. "Weren't you happy when we were watching that movie?" That was okay *then*, Eric explains, but this is now. "Now, it's enough." He begins to move, putting weight onto his right hand in a way that suggests he's getting ready to swing his legs out from under the bedspread and onto the floor. Then, all at once, he disappears. It's as if he evaporated.

For many years of our adult lives we sat together in bed like this, side by side, reading the newspaper. The difference is, it would be early morning, not nighttime, the paper recently delivered, a piece of the world hurled onto our porch in St. Louis or dropped at the edge of our front yard in Vermont, requiring me to make a trek in my pajamas to retrieve it. Papers are delivered by people in automobiles now, often old people with disabilities, not like the paperboy of my childhood, with a strong throwing arm and good aim.

Meanwhile, Mark Trail never gets a day older, from day to day, from week to week, from year to year—at least not based on the way he looks in the comic strip, one of the sweet pleasures my husband and I used to share every morning in St. Louis, where it appears daily in the *Post Dispatch*.

I can't remember the last time Eric and I sat together in bed that way, sharing the paper. There had been a story involving Mark hiking in the Himalayas with a man named Dr. Camel who claimed to have lost his leg in a yeti attack, his prosthesis coming as a great surprise to everyone despite the fact that they seemed to have been hiking together for days, nor was it clear why there was a glamorous dark-haired woman named Genie hiking with them. We always encountered a *Mark Trail* narrative midstream, since our Vermont paper doesn't carry the daily strip, only a large Sunday panel devoted to describing the usually malevolent behavior of a specific animal, the African elephant, for instance (shown tossing a hapless villager into the air), or the difference between an antler and a horn. But the hiking story seemed to be ending and another story—something focused on Mark and Cherry's little boy, Rusty, who looked like he was growing older, practically a teenager with an interest in girls—just getting started.

When someone you have lived with for a very long time dies, memory stops working its regular way—it goes crazy. It is no longer like remembering; it is, more often, like astral projection. "Like darkness in the movies, it tests the outline of your astral footprint," my subconscious mind informed me the other night, speaking from beyond the bedroom wall, whereas the great memoirist Chateaubriand, speaking from beyond the grave, observed sourly that memory is often a quality associated with stupidity.

I first saw the knight on a class trip to the Cloisters my senior year in high school. Springtime, the trees along the parkway leafing out—romance was in the air, along with hints of restlessness and dread. It's amazing how you see the places you're headed in life ahead of time and have no idea that's what's happening. Death awaits you, you've been told. This is the fundamental fact of being alive and yet you try to jump across it. Eric had been reading the paper, and whatever he'd been reading, he was getting impatient. If Mark Trail remained the same age while Rusty kept getting older, eventually Rusty would bypass him. Mark would still be middle-aged, and Rusty would be an old man, getting older and older until at last he died.

In the Cloisters people trod softly. They spoke in hushed voices but even so their words echoed everywhere; it was as if the past was speaking, as if it issued from the smell of the place, water dripping on stone. I could stand by myself—enamored of the thought of myself, alone, standing there, sufficient unto myself—staring down at the effigy of Jean d'Alluye, the French Crusader knight, more handsome by far than the boy in my class I'd thought I had such a crush on and yet, somehow, both of them similar by virtue of their inaccessibility. Boys, then, were wearing their hair longer but they also had bangs. The knight's flowing locks left his forehead elegantly bare; he wore a chain-mail shirt, and folded his hands piously above his breastbone in exact replication of the knight at the beginning of *The Seventh Seal*, moments before he meets up with Death. There was a lion resting at Jean d'Alluye's feet that our teacher had told us signified courage. He also told us, erroneously, that crossed legs signified death in battle.

That teacher is dead now. He probably didn't know that the knight's sword came, surprisingly, from China, or that the effigy of the knight, facedown, had served for a period of time following the French Revolution as a bridge over a small stream outside of Tours, watching the little fish swim by below. Of course the knight himself was no longer there to watch anything; whatever was left of him had been summarily disposed of by the sansculottes. We read "The Knight's Tale" in the original Middle English in that teacher's class. "Love is a gretter lawe, by my pan / Than may be yeve to any erthely man; / And therefore positif lawe and swich decree / Is broken al day for love in ech degree." The words barely hovered at the thin edge of familiarity, not unlike the overwhelming beauty of the knight's face, thoughts forming behind it in a mind of stone.

Eventually we were on the bus going home. It was dark; I was sitting beside the crush who, amazingly, had decided to take the seat next to me. The darkness of the bus was nothing like the darkness of the Gothic Chapel where Jean d'Alluye lay on his back, his eyes wide open, staring up at the ribbed vault of the ceiling for all eternity. Some of my classmates had lit the little lights above their seats but the crush and I kept ours unlit, his intentions perhaps having been amorous, whereas mine were to sink deeper into the darkness, made darker still by the intermittent lights appearing out the window once we'd left the city behind. In those days it was a three-hour ride from New York City to

Philadelphia. The boys sitting behind us had brought whiskey in a flask. I could smell it, the smell of cocktail hour on Woodale Road. I don't live here, I thought. I am not here. In the Gothic Chapel the only light had come from outdoors through the stained glass double lancet windows. It was hard to see anything, really. When we first came into the room there had been a single large candle in a candle stand in the corner, but at some point the candle had gotten blown out.

Shaken, not stirred, the crush said, accepting the flask from the seat behind us. Bond, replied one of the two boys, James Bond. The candle had gone out and the wick was still glowing, emitting the trail of smoke our teacher told us signified the presence of the Holy Ghost, the most mysterious and hence most terrible (as in causing terror, awe, or dread) aspect of the Trinity. Outside the window the lights of apartment buildings loomed near the highway, the shapes of trees, the great heaving bodies of the willows.

The boys were talking about Dr. No's metal hands. They were his Achilles heel, the crush said, solemnly, and I knew, just as well as I would ever know anything in the course of my long and fiercely cherished life, that nothing would ever be sufficient. "The proof that the little prince existed is that he was charming, that he laughed, and that he was looking for a sheep," my adored sixth-grade teacher, Mr. Fine, had read to us, and my adored sixth-grade crush, Eddie Williams, had rolled his eyes.

The point is, a crush goes nowhere. It's called a crush because something landed on top of you, making movement impossible. It isn't the same as a love affair that—whether star-crossed or blest—confers motion, ferrying you through time. There you are, crushed, the sole stirring of life in you occasioned by the sight of the crushing object, no matter the grace of its limbs or lightness of spirit. And, truly, what is the point? In terms of the future of the planet, for example.

On the bus back from New York City I courted the terror, the whole span of what it is like to be born, to fall in love, to love someone and live a life with them and then at the very tail end of it encounter death. The dark room, the great dark vaulted ceiling. "Four suns hung in the afternoon sky," sang the squire, following his knight across the plague-ridden landscape. "But if the sheep eats the flower," Mr. Fine read, "then for him it's as if, suddenly, all the stars went out," and Eddie Williams doubled over laughing. I wanted to be alone more than anything and I wanted to be in love. I wanted the entire *history* of it, not just a lifetime but something vaster, infinite even, except not *really* infinite since infinity was too frightening. "Because I know just as well as I'm standing here talking to you," sang Peggy Lee, "that when that final moment comes . . ." And the seven angels who had the seven trumpets prepared themselves to sound.

Vigilance

It began as a joke. My husband was dying. He had only so much time left—how much, we didn't know. His spirits were generally good, and the shingles virus that made his last days miserable had yet to emerge from its hiding place deep in his body, meaning we could still share the same bed and spend our mornings side by side, drinking coffee and looking at the local paper, all ten pages of it. Personal details about your private life are made public today, my husband said, reading the horoscope. Meanwhile you need more sleep.

The bedroom has four large windows, facing east, direction of the rising sun, the waxing moon, Rabbit, Air, Redemption. The way the house is situated, on a small rise above the street, what you see out the bedroom windows are the branches of locust trees framing pieces of sky shaped like jigsaw puzzle pieces, the kind I had as a girl where some pieces are shaped like things, a horn, a bicycle wheel, a bird, a shoe. My favorite showed a scene with birds standing one-legged in a marsh at sunset, the sun sending all sorts of colors across the black water. It made no sense for a high-heeled shoe to be there. This is what I was thinking while my dying husband read me my horoscope.

And the wind. And the drops of rain like bullets. Gros Morne, the final pitch a sheer wall of scree and there it was, at the foot of the wall, dropped on the talus, a red high-heeled shoe. It hardly makes sense to think about how it got there, or how I did, for that matter. I was a girl who constructed forts out of bedsheets in the living room—that was as close as I came to a tent, and my idea of mountains came from a movie I saw on our tiny black-and-white television screen about men climbing the Matterhorn. The Matterhorn had a pointed top exactly like the mountains we were taught to draw in school. "It shook you off like lice," an old woman pointed out to the climbers, after the avalanche chased them back down to the village.

It was at about this time that my friend Alex and his wife bought a house in The Hague, a charming brick row house with a balcony and chimney pots, and when I showed my husband the picture he said it made him sad that after all the money and work we'd put into our house—and he enumerated, bookshelves, stone walls, bookshelves, walls, shelves! shelves! (for over the years we'd come to own many books we were loath to part with, most recently my husband's complete collection of Rex Stout mysteries, a talismanic obsession that had grown in tandem with the cancer)—after all that, my husband said, not to mention the tortured beech out front, a baby when we planted it and just think of it now, casting its tortuous shadow far and wide across the lawn, how could he dream of leaving? He stared at me intently, the dark brown of his irises more transparent, like he was letting me see inside his head.

Inside my husband's head was an idea, and the idea had its origins in his background as an ecological economist. Limitless growth is bad. Processes that involve the transfer or conversion of energy are irreversible.

Ruth says the city's infrastructure is in worse shape than I am, my husband went on to say. Though by this time he'd stopped joining me on the daily dog walk in Hubbard Park, until recently he'd managed to maintain the ritual by taking a shortcut that avoided the steep uphill climb through a lichen-shrouded ravine. We would find him sitting in the sun on a table in the Seven Fireplaces (of which I've never been able to count more than five) picnic area, the dogs, having raced ahead of us, sitting at his feet staring up at him, our Lucy and Susan's Reilly and Betty's Walnut and

Ruth's little Maya. It was simple enough to conflate Ruth's view of our sewer system with the occult data on the disks routinely handed to us by the good-natured medical personnel whose job it was to keep track of the story unfolding inside my husband's organs. There was a narrative involved that didn't follow conventional rules, unlike those governing Rex Stout, just as the work being done on the sewer system (the road torn up every day and the rubble dumped back in at night) seemed like the project of insane elves.

But you don't have to leave the house, I said. You could haunt it.

The imperative to be vigilant is always there, it's only that there are times in the life of a person or the world when it seems more crucial. Just as there are limits to what vigilance can achieve.

At some point during the election year of 1956, my father gave me a beautiful glossy sticker that said I LIKE IKE. I affixed it to the center of the top drawer of my maple dresser, knowing as I did so that in our family to put a sticker on a piece of furniture was akin to putting a sticker on my little sister. "I can't believe you did that," my mother said. Shortly thereafter she gave me a beautiful glossy sticker that said MADLY FOR ADLAI. I was ten years old; I had written a get-well card to Eisenhower a year earlier when he had a heart attack, and to my amazement I'd gotten a thank you card back that my best friend Peggy's older brother Marto said hadn't actually been signed by Mamie Eisenhower. "That's just printed on," Marto said.

I still have the maple dresser and the maple bed. The bed has tooth marks along the headboard where I chewed on it when I couldn't sleep. In 1956 my job was to keep vigil over the night sky for the plane that was carrying the bomb that was going to turn us all to bone and then to ash and then to nothing. The dresser sat across from the bed and next to the console radio set to 1190 AM WOWO, Fort Wayne, Indiana, "the voice of a thousand main streets," that somehow managed to be everywhere, all at once, all night long. My job was to listen to the radio whenever I heard a siren, making sure the world wasn't about to end.

For many years the two stickers coexisted on the dresser drawer, IKE in the center and ADLAI to the left. At night while I kept vigil they were companions to me, their twin presence reassuring, the eyes of a single deity lit by the light of the 23 trolley as it made its way up and down Germantown Avenue. Nowadays the dresser is on the third floor, in my daughter's old bedroom, a place where things get put on their way to the yard sale. Considering its age, the dresser's overall finish is in good shape, the top drawer noticeably scuffed in the area between the drawer pulls where at some point I scraped off the stickers.

What was I thinking? I no longer needed them? By the time I was the girl in the tent in the rain at the foot of Gros

Morne I had traded vigilance for romance. I had done some traveling, yes, but always to places where a person stayed in a building of some kind and slept in a bed, even if on a damp Greek mattress. In the house where I grew up, furniture was coin of the realm. All our furniture had names: highboy, bachelor chest, piecrust table. I had never courted danger. Whereas my old boyfriend was scornful of trail markers. Like the hero of *The Challenge*—the 1938 movie about the first ascent of the Matterhorn that I'd watched sitting in the wing chair in the family living room on Woodale Road—he always preferred to take the impossible route to the summit, and to execute the endeavor, even if it was doomed, with style.

I never imagined myself atop a mountain in Newfoundland. But then I didn't imagine myself in bed with a dying husband, either.

In the bardo, narrative seems to happen but doesn't. You think you are making a tuna sandwich. You think you are cutting the tuna sandwich into little squares to tempt your dying husband's appetite. We're born into the life bardo, and when we begin to die we're in the dying bardo, and after that we're in the death bardo, at which point we make our transition back via rebirth into the birth bardo, having experienced delight in the meeting between sperm and ovum and from that state of bliss fainting into unconsciousness and, as time passes, coming to maturity in the womb until finally, emerging from the womb and opening our eyes, we will have turned into a puppy or something and are back once again in the life bardo.

The idea is that you are not supposed to encourage a dead person to stay with you. You are not supposed to encourage a haunting, to cause someone you love to get stuck here in this, this most insufferable of the bardos.

"Oh you, with your mind far away, thinking that death will not come, / Entranced by the pointless activities of this life, / If you were to return empty-handed now, would not your life's purpose have been utterly confused?" So the lama is instructed to address the deceased person in the *Tibetan Book of the Dead*, urging him to move on. "O (Name of deceased)! Listen carefully!"

"O Eric! Listen carefully!"

Afterward I found the bookmark he left in the Rex Stout mystery, midway through the book, the sentence "The bag slipped from her hand to the floor and her face went white and stiff" at the top of the page. I thought of Eric's dark brown eyes moving across the page and then growing tired. The vitreous humor. And then.

And then the road bent left. "I had seen people turn pale before, but I had never seen blood leave skin so thoroughly and so fast," the book went on to say. I dreamed I was picking red flowers. To the right, a large tree of some kind beginning to leaf out, one gray asbestos wall of the general store visible behind it. We had just met. By summer the green Valvoline advertisement no longer in view. The eyes staring fixedly without blinking. The scaling of the mountain of the elements. Place the wrist at the point between the eyebrows. The arm so thin as to be a line and then it was gone.

The Haunted Tent

You make a long pole by fitting together several short poles that are connected inside by a single strand of elastic. The long poles get fed through color-coded casings. Then you stand the whole thing up, unless the person feeding the poles through hasn't done the job correctly, in which case there is no tent, just a pile of green fabric lying on the ground. Sometimes the tent stands up perfectly but the tent pegs can't be hammered in because the person who picked the tent site failed to notice that it's (a) solid rock, or (b) nothing but sand, in which case a strong wind could blow the whole thing away. These could be two different people. Maybe they have a little daughter they've sent off to fill the water jug. The glass has bottomed out, the wind is freshening. Meat Cove isn't an auspicious name for a campsite.

I don't think this is why my parents hated the idea of sleeping in a tent. I think my parents resisted with every fiber of their being the idea of getting taken off guard, which is to say that they approached all change as an opportunity to exercise their talent for denial—which is also to say that's why cocktail hour came earlier every day. There is nothing more reliable than cocktail hour: it begins at what appears to be a regular time and always involves drinking cocktails, at which point life's uncertainties simply melt away.

Life in a tent is nothing if not one surprise after another. You might go to sleep on an uninhabited plot of campground and awaken to find yourself surrounded by a circle of moonlit skunks. Rain might pound through the tent fly, and thence onto your sleeping body. A total stranger might come walking in, having mistaken your tent for his.

Quite late in life my husband discovered he wasn't part Hungarian, as he'd thought, but Croatian. When he asked one of his newfound Croatian relatives what Croatians are known for (as Italians are known for lovemaking, the French for superciliousness, my people for drunkenness and verbosity), his relative said, Croatians like fighting, and, truly, my husband inherited a bad temper from his Croatian forebears, whereas I had opted early on for sainthood—though, to be honest, I didn't get off to a flying start. When the boy on the mat next to mine at nap time gave me a card he'd got at church that had a picture on it of Saint Catherine—not spelled the way it was supposed to be spelled—holding her wheel like a pet, I pinched him until he called Mrs. Patterson and she made me sit under the sink. When temper unfurls it unfurls like a banner. Temper is the banner the righteous carry into battle.

Meanwhile at Meat Cove, tent life wasn't going well. I was fighting the wind to get the camp stove going; my husband was trying to make a campfire. Our daughter had returned with the water and was hungry. We had arrived later than planned due to a delayed ferry crossing. Okay, I said. Let me see if I can get this thing to work. A sign told us we needed to lock our food in the car because of bears. Meat Cove, Meat Cove. The wood they sold at the camp store had been cut from saplings, my husband said. I wouldn't believe the disgusting crap the slobs who'd had our site before us left in the firepit. It was the bears, said our daughter. No, I said, the propane tank is almost empty. Did you hear what I said? My husband kicked the side of the firepit. Why do you start every sentence with "no"? Have you seen the bug spray? I asked. I never listened; that was the whole problem with me. Our daughter needed to pee. A car filled with young people pulled into the site next to ours, the radio turned up all the way. *Here I go again on my own, goin' down the only road I've ever known . . .* At some point we must have eaten something resembling dinner, after which the three of us sat around the picnic table swatting mosquitoes. Then our daughter went to bed and the mosquitoes left and we lit the propane lamp and the moths arrived. Whiskey and cigarettes and gin rummy—it was like throwing gasoline on a fire. The tent just sat there, too, taking it in. Physical bodies do that. Then it began to rain.

That's the thing about camping; if you want to get away, there's nowhere to go. The fly had come loose and was flapping against the tent. A tent isn't like an old house with a history; a ghost can't just rise up out of nothing. I wish I was dead, I said. I tried to say it softly so as not to wake our daughter. Then the angry ghost came out of me and joined the angry ghost of my husband. Where his head emerged from the top of his sleeping bag I could see his eyeballs shining, meaning he was awake.

People talk about someone having the patience of a saint. In the sixth century, a young monk named Dositheus was assigned to care for the sick members of the community. The self-centeredness to which illness sometimes gives rise can make people unreasonable in their demands; when this happened in the monastery, Dositheus would lose his temper and scream and yell at the sick monks, until, filled with remorse, he'd run to his cell, throw himself on the floor, weep bitter tears, and beg God's mercy. "Look how well I have made the beds!" Dositheus pointed out, and God replied, "You are an excellent bed-maker, no doubt, but I fear not much of a monk." Dositheus eventually became so kind, patient, and cheerful that those who were sick loved having him around—and so, he was made into a saint.

Meanwhile at Meat Cove the external trappings of rage were flying around the physical bodies lying inside our tent. *Like a drifter I was born to walk alone, and I've made up my mind, I ain't wasting no more time* . . . Our tent, the tent next door, all the other tents. *Here I go again, here I go again, ooh baby* . . . Whitesnake, said my husband. I don't fucking believe this. Then he turned on his CPAP machine and drowned everything out.

For every human being who has ever dwelt upon this planet the great mystery never changes: Who is the immortal beloved? My best friend Peggy's mother always said there had never been man born to woman to compare with Peggy's father, but then why did we sometimes catch a glimpse of her seated at her vanity bench, brushing and brushing her long brown hair and crying? You must suffer to be beautiful, she told us and I knew I had a lot of suffering in store. Besides, Mr. Lentz could be cruel. He had killed Germans during the war—that was the explanation—but also he revered Camus, who'd said, "If it were sufficient to love, things would be too easy."

And, really, the greater mystery is, given the tremendous risk of error in the choice of womb entrance, due to the state of total bewilderment at the moment of death, the experience of being pursued by whirlwinds, blizzards, hail or fog, as well as a large crowd of other dead people, why did Mr. Lentz end up in his body, and not in Peggy's? Why did my husband end up in his body, and our daughter in hers?

Not to mention me, consigned at six o'clock in the morning of the thirteenth of November to the body of a girl baby in the city of Philadelphia in the middle years of the twentieth century—a young girl with excellent hearing, it must be admitted, bringing to my awakening soul the sounds of a dog lapping water from his water bowl, a trolley car on its way toward the excitingly named yet ultimately disappointing Mermaid Trolley Loop, a Louisville Slugger bat making contact with a softball, a hiccup. I was prone to hiccups, as well as to night terrors, my screaming as I slipped through a hole in the fabric of the known world and down the moist gullet of the universe enough to make everyone around me wish for my return, once again, to the luminous bardo of *dharmata*, where I'd be kept so busy trying to figure out a way to obstruct the womb entrances and not get forever cast back into one of the six classes of beings, as a dachshund or a parakeet, a hell being or a moth, a hungry ghost or a human child with the black hair of her French grandmother and the green eyes of no one in particular, that I'd finally stop screaming.

How was this placement determined and by whom? Following my sojourn in the bardo I was no more knowledgeable about these matters than I'd been before, though it is true that roaming in the intermediate state of rebirth was one of the great joys of my life. But why did some people get a body that lasted a long time, and some people didn't?

For a while, my immortal beloved had been Beethoven. That much I knew, and that even the Swedish boy who entered our class just after Thanksgiving and who claimed to be in love with me was nothing by comparison. The wish to attach oneself to greatness comes early; it's corollary to the wish to be great, which is a wish better kept to oneself if one happens to be an American girl suffering to be a beautiful pianist on a suburban street in Philadelphia right after the end of the Second World War. He could be a lamb, Beethoven, but he could also be a monster. He threw hot food at a waiter; he swept candles off a piano during a bad performance; he hit a choirboy. He became embroiled in a bitter custody battle for a nephew who attempted suicide to escape the family animosity. "Composers do not cry," Beethoven said. "Composers are made of fire."

According to Marto—another of my immortal beloveds— the Second World War had destroyed his father, Mr. Lentz. "Why do you think he spends all his time napping?" Marto asked. I'd pretended that after I'd gotten up onto the roof of the Lentzes' garage I couldn't get down, necessitating rescue, but we both saw through that ruse. "Because he's tired?" Marto smiled, breaking my heart. I was young and stupid and Marto spent his weekends living in sin with a Sarah Lawrence student. "He has shell shock," Marto said. "My father will never be a whole person." "If he ever was," said Henry Lee, son of the cruel pediatrician, who had appeared as if from out of nowhere in his homemade

Superman cape. He crossed his eyes and made a bubbling sound with his overlarge annoying lips.

It was said that Beethoven's bagatelle *Für Elise* had been written for his student Therese Malfatti—he had terrible handwriting, which is why future musicologists misread the name. Beethoven fell in love with his student and, as with so many of his affairs of the heart, the love was unrequited. Therese was twenty years younger than he was, for starters. Plus there was his famous bad temper. The only happy outcome of the situation—aside from the bagatelle, butchered by beginning piano students the world over— was the way Therese's little dog, Gigons, took a shine to the sorrowful composer and followed him home through the darkening streets of Vienna. What kind of dog was Gigons? No one seems to know. But I'm thinking a dachshund, a German dog. Nor did Mrs. Gerson, my piano teacher, permit any of her students to play *Für Elise*. Let's leave well enough alone, she said, when I complained.

Dog Walk

A dog can be off leash in Hubbard Park assuming its owner has the dog under control, but who's to say what constitutes control? In early spring when the snow melts the deer carcasses emerge, beckoning to the dogs the way the bells of the ice cream truck do to human children, at which time my darling dog races along with the other dogs into the frozen waste, reappearing with a giant bone clamped between her teeth. There's no way you can pry those jaws apart. She doesn't growl; she's using all the energy she has to hold on tight. Someone's house had a tree fall on it during that wind last night, says one of the dog walkers. Someone left his wife for the Pilates instructor, says another, and when we demand details she makes the locked lips sign. Grace Paley said gossip is a neighborhood's way of developing a moral sense, but it's also a way of establishing dominance.

As long as Eric was walking with us it wasn't like junior high. Anyone who thinks a world run by women would be a safer, saner place has never spent time with girls. Occasionally it happened that Mr. Fine took the three of us classmates— his pets—to Kaybak's drugstore after school. He was lithe, impatient, his dark hair combed back to reveal the slightest widow's peak high on his forehead. Robespierre Ichabod Fine—he told us his mother had named him after her heroes. I think Mr. Fine's energy was largely sensual but I was impervious to the clues; I was twelve going on a hundred. Rosemary informed me (in the same spirit with which she'd told me I had bad breath) that I should stop ordering milkshakes because they were not only expensive but fattening, whereas Liz laughed flirtatiously and made a lot of noise with her straw.

Though, really, competition doesn't begin to describe what goes on with girls; it's a fight to the death, and the prize isn't always a boyfriend. There's only room for one girl to be most beautiful, just as there's only room for one to be smartest or most athletic. More to the point, only one girl gets to be right. Are the unsightly silken tents on the trees caused by tentworms or webworms? Tentworms come in the spring. Everyone knows those are gypsy moths. And what about the new signposts? Just look at them! What's so bad about making the park friendlier for visitors? Nothing, if you think hideousness is friendly. Plus, who dreamed up those names? Eric's presence among us was a little like what happens when you drop an egg white "raft" into stock to clarify it.

It was our house he was supposed to haunt, but the Seven Fireplaces is where I sometimes see him. Now, more than a year after his death, Lucy will take off from what one of the new signposts calls the Streamside Roundabout Trail, racing up a steep hillside to what another new signpost calls the Cliffside Trail, where we find her sitting by the picnic table, panting and waiting, though waiting isn't usually a feeling we connect with walking. Walking is a way of avoiding having to wait.

Lucy has always loved men more than women; I could never take it personally that she preferred Eric. Once he was dying she wouldn't let him out of her sight.

"I walked through the mountains today. The weather was damp, and the entire region was gray. But the road was soft and in places very clean. At first I had my coat on; soon, however, I pulled it off, folded it together, and laid it upon my arm. The walk on the wonderful road gave me more and ever more pleasure; first it went up and then descended again."

Robert Walser wrote over fifty stories about walking; this is from "A Little Ramble," one of the shortest of these, and like all Walser's prose, impossible to categorize, though Susan Sontag ("a cross between Stevie Smith and Beckett") tried. Walser's stories about walking are considered fiction, yet it's clear the narrator is the same person as the author. "Walk . . . I definitely must, to invigorate myself and to maintain contact with the living world, without perceiving which I could not write the half of one more single word. . . . Without walking I would be dead."

Hubbard Park is big, over two hundred acres. It's more of a forest than a park, its trail system the lightest overlay; when you climb to the top of the stone tower all you see spreading out at your feet are trees, great stands of Norway spruce and red pine, restless outcroppings of beech, dark blue-green pockets of hemlock. There's a map, but it isn't very informative. Anything might be down there, porcupines, skunks, bears. A fisher cat, mouth agape, razor-sharp teeth bared and ready to bite. One day I came upon a woman who turned out to be from Russia, wearing a red duffle coat and standing on a stone in the middle of the brook where the lady's slippers come up each spring. She was crying, clearly lost and furious.

Every day we follow the same route, along the wide path from the park entrance and then into the woods. Every day is the same except for the weather, which is always different, and except for the dogs, whose priorities are not the same as ours.

.Sometimes it happens that when the dogs run off, your dog is the one that doesn't come back. You call and call, promising treats that the other dogs, feigning obedience, happily consume. At some point there's nothing left to do but head off trail, leaving behind your friends and the friendly sound of their voices calling *Lucy, Lucy,* as all the while the wind is picking up, the trees bending side to side, making groaning sounds, hurling parts of themselves to the ground. Is it worse to not know where your dog is or where you are, yourself? The birds, for example—what has become of them? It used to be there were birds everywhere. That flash of something unseen from the corner of your eye—it didn't need to manifest itself to let you know that where you are isn't any place you've been before, the world's surface a mess like it's been from the beginning, tree roots and stones underfoot—until, all at once, a blade of sun! ice-melt dripping from an overhanging tree onto deadfall, and up ahead a dark shape like a stone perched on a picnic table, slightly hunched and unrecognizable, Lucy on the ground at its feet.

Once I persuaded Eric to accompany me to a Buddhist temple hidden in the woods in the middle of nowhere, which is to say not far from the white farmhouse where we lived together when we first fell in love. The monk would introduce us to the practices of *zazen* and *kinhin,* I explained. I hoped the visit would prove restorative, while at the same time secretly nursing the conviction—having forgotten how my husband was always more graceful by far than I was—that I was going to be best at both these practices.

Kinhin—or walking meditation—is a common Buddhist practice, meaning to *go through* like the thread on a loom, or (literally) to walk straight back and forth. Walking meditation involves thinking about and executing a series of actions you normally do without thinking. You begin by lifting one foot, moving it slightly forward and setting it on the floor, heel first, then shifting the weight of your body onto the forward leg as the back heel lifts, the toes remaining on the ground until you completely lift the foot, observing it as it swings forward and lowers, making contact with the ground, heel first, your weight shifting onto that foot as your body moves forward.

I used to like to take my portable record player with me and sit on the living room floor behind the wing chair between the piecrust table and the grandfather clock. I think it is true the music you hear when you are a child is the music you hear inside your ears your whole life long. Back then I was enamored of *Peter and the Wolf*—we had a boxed set of three red 78 rpm records, narrated by a man with one of those vaguely British accents Americans liked to use to sound cultured. "Early one morning Peter opened the garden gate and went out into a big green meadow." Peter's grandfather had told him never to open the gate, but the music suggested this wouldn't prove disastrous, the melody lilting, carried by the strings. In the end, the only unfortunate thing that happened was the wolf ate the duck, though it wasn't supposed to be sad despite the heartbreaking sound of the oboe, because the wolf swallowed the duck whole—as if life inside a wolf wasn't such a bad thing.

Eric was my husband. In the beginning he took me away from myself. He could even make me look like a good dancer. I wanted other things—I was wildly ambitious—but those things required acts of will and were consequently subject to judgment, whereas the transformative power of marriage operated by magic. When I assigned Peter's theme to Eric's ringtone it was because that was the spirit with which he set out into the park every morning—set out anywhere, really.

It's almost impossible to see a small child sitting on the floor behind a wing chair; you could listen to a record and not be bothered. You could recite "The Janitor's Boy," and "Ozymandias" and not be asked what you were doing. You could cry about the duck. You could disappear, as if disappearance is a choice.

The Elder-Tree Mother

"There was once a little boy who had taken cold by going out and getting his feet wet," the tale begins. "No one could think how he had managed to do so, for the weather was quite dry . . ." You didn't have to be a genius to see that this was the way I'd come down with pleurisy at my best friend Peggy's seventh birthday party, or to realize that the black gumdrop and toothpick poodle I'd been making was to blame. So it happened that I got to spend the whole next month in bed, my mother beside me, reading me one fairy tale after another. Every now and then she'd steal a glance in my direction to make sure I hadn't stopped breathing.

Downstairs the sun may have been shining, my little sister playing her Mouse Guitar, my father whistling, the dachshund racing mindlessly from one end of the house to the other. Downstairs it may have been noisy and bright but upstairs in my bedroom it was hushed and dark. My mother had drawn the venetian blinds and plugged in the raveling black-and-white cord of the vaporizer, a queerly shaped enamel-coated relic of her own sickly childhood. Puffs of yellow steam came out of a hole in its top, musty and stale smelling, as if the steam itself were a thing of the past. "The little boy looked at the teapot and saw the lid raise itself gradually. Branches sprouted, even from the spout, in all directions, till they became larger and larger, and there appeared a large elder tree, covered with flowers white and fresh . . ."

Hans Christian Andersen goes on to describe an old man and woman on the eve of their golden wedding anniversary, sitting under an elder tree, reminiscing. Long ago when they were children, long before the man sailed away and the woman pined for the letters he sent "from the land where the coffee berries grew," long before he came back to her and they had children and grandchildren and great-grandchildren, they planted the twig that became a tree. "'That is not a story,'" complains the little sick boy, reasonably enough, to which the Elder-Tree Mother replies, "'Not exactly, but the story is coming now, and it is a true one. For out of the truth grow the most wonderful stories, just as my elder bush has sprung out of the teapot.'" Then she takes the boy on a journey through his own life, season after season, year after year, in the course of which he grows older and older—until he realizes that *he* is the old man celebrating his golden anniversary. "And the two old people sat in the red glow of the evening sunlight, and closed their eyes, and—and—the story was ended." Meanwhile the Elder-Tree Mother (whose name is Memory) has remained a beautiful young girl. Where is she now? the boy wants to know. "She is in the teapot," his mother tells him. "And there she may stay."

How clearly Andersen expressed my dawning sense of what it meant to be mortal. One day, before I even suspected what was happening, I'd be very old, at death's door (as those stuttering *and*s suggested), and I'd remember myself as a seven-year-old girl lying in a dark room in a maple bed, her mother (who'd have died years earlier) jumping up to begin dinner, leaving her alone with a vaporizer. Unless you were a goddess and immortal, youth was no proof against death. Though it was less Andersen's view of mortality than his genius for conjuring a sense of time—of what constitutes the span of a human life—that I couldn't get enough of, couldn't remove my eyes from even for a second, like a spider crossing the ceiling right above your head.

In those days I had two editions of Andersen, the forest-green 1945 Grosset & Dunlap with the disturbing Arthur Szyk illustrations, and the baby-blue 1946 Rainbow Classic, with Jean O'Neill's insanely sweet-faced rendering of the Snow Queen. I thought that was the extent of my childhood collection until my friend Alexandra gave me a boxed edition for my birthday, causing Memory (still infuriatingly young) to leap all at once from her hiding place in the teapot.

Manufactured in 1950 by the Nordic Paper Industry of Jutland, Denmark, the set of twelve tiny volumes is housed in a slightly larger box with a picture on the cover of three incongruously American-looking children listening to a thin fellow in a frock coat read to them in front of a lopsided castle. The cover's doors open to reveal a second pair of doors in a majestic mahogany cupboard, and behind that set of doors a recessed shelf containing "Little Ida's Flowers," "The Happy Family," "The Wild Swans," "The Steadfast Tin Soldier" . . .

"He seemed a little different as he had been cast last of all. The tin was short so he had only one leg. . . . On the table were many other playthings, and one that no eye could miss was a marvelous castle of cardboards . . . but prettiest of all was the little paper dancer who stood in the doorway with a dainty blue ribbon over her shoulders, set off by a brilliant spangle." The Nordic Paper Industry's translator wisely chooses to remain anonymous, unlike Mrs. E. V. Lucas and Mrs. H. B. Paull (translators of the Grosset & Dunlap edition), who offer instead: "There was not quite enough tin left," and "a delightful paper castle." And while the solecisms themselves don't ring any bells, there's no doubt in my mind that the memory summoned by the picture on the tiny book's cover—a row of soldiers standing at attention, oblivious to the goblin who has popped from his home in the snuffbox to engineer the soldier's tragic fate—is not only real but pristine, a memory I didn't even know I'd forgotten.

I can smell Vicks and Lipton noodle soup, hear my father tiptoeing closer—is she awake? yes!—and then shyly handing me a package containing a similar set of books. Maybe even this precise set, banished to the cellar with the Mouse Guitar and then dispatched after my father's stroke (along with the venetian blinds and the vaporizer) to the Christmas bazaar at St. Martin-in-the-Fields where it was bought by a maiden aunt for her niece who one day likewise grew too old and traded it for a copy of *The Spoils of Poynton* at the used-book shop where my friend Alexandra found it hidden under a pile of topo maps.

"The Steadfast Tin Soldier" ends when a young man ("without rhyme or reason . . . no doubt the goblin in the snuffbox was to blame") throws the tin soldier into the stove, and a breeze blows the paper dancer in after it. "When the maid took away the ashes the next morning, she found the soldier in the shape of a little tin heart. But of the pretty dancer nothing was left except her spangle, and that was burned as black as coal."

A dancer inside a castle inside a book inside a bookcase inside a cupboard inside a castle-studded landscape: how deftly the Nordic Paper Industry managed to convey the terror I knew lurked at the heart of the Christian message. Your tenure on this earth, where you might prefer to stay (despite its perils, the perverse machinery of cause and effect embodied in snuffbox goblins and gumdrop poodles), would be finite, yet once you died you'd have no choice but to go on forever and ever. You had only to imagine a door, the door through which you couldn't step, and the next thing you knew that door would be opening and behind it would be . . . another door! And another!

The Marsh King's daughter returns from "a moment" in heaven to find that the stork she was talking to moments earlier hasn't any idea who she is. "'Yes,'" the stork says, "'there certainly was a princess in Egypt who came from the Danish land, but she disappeared on her wedding night many hundreds of years ago. You may read all about it on the monument in the garden. There are both storks and swans carved there, and you are at the top yourself, all in white marble.'"

"'On your very first evening!'" the mother of the winds scolds the prince. "'I thought as much. If you were my boy, you should go into the bag!'" To which Death replies, "'Ah, he shall, soon enough! When he least expects me, I shall come back, lay him in a black coffin, put it on my head, and fly to the skies. The Garden of Paradise blooms there, too, and if he is good and holy he shall enter into it. But if his thoughts are wicked and his heart still full of sin, he will sink deeper in his coffin than Paradise sank. And I shall go only once every thousand years to see if he is to sink deeper or rise to the stars—the bright stars up there.'"

I believed these were my stories. Mine. I didn't think they'd been written for me, Andersen having "had me in mind," or that they conveyed my view of things with unusual precision—no, when I heard these stories I was infused with that shiver of ecstasy that is an unmistakable symptom of the creative act. I felt as if I'd created the stories, as if they had their origin in my imagination, as if they were by definition my original work, having "belonged at the beginning to the person in question," that person being me.

I'm not referring to plot. In fact plot was the least of it. I'm referring to individual words, phrases. *Black as coal. Goblin. Spangle. Snuffbox.*

When I was seven years old I didn't have a clue what a snuffbox was, but I knew it was the right name for an object that sprang open unexpectedly to release a goblin. Later it would come as no surprise that Benny Trimble, who lived down the street from us and was said to use snuff, set fire to his mother's house by smoking in bed.

In the country of Hjørring, high up toward the Skaw in the
  north of Jutland.
She is in the teapot, and there she may stay.
The storks have a great many stories which they tell their
  little ones, all about the bogs and the marshes.

Once every thousand years.

Kribble krabble. Skaw. Jutland.

Into the bag! The bright stars up there!

There was nothing passive about this experience. Even now, typing Andersen's words and his sentences, I can feel a ghost of that first ecstatic shiver. This wasn't like being a reader, not even the kind of reader a writer eventually becomes, studying, dismantling, pilfering. This was primal, this sensation, and not unlike the doomed prince in "The Garden of Paradise"—who isn't satisfied merely to dance with the fairy but goes on to kiss her despite all the warnings—it released in me a heedless spirit, a desire not only to leave Hans Christian Andersen behind, but to leave him annihilated.

When I tried rereading "The Elder-Tree Mother" it was as if the story had turned to a block of ice my eyes were forced to slide across. The idea of reading the story, that it had once played a key role in my life, continued on some level to interest me, but there was nothing seductive about the story itself. I felt a version of the frantic repulsion I feel when someone reads over my shoulder; more than that, I felt something akin to fury at the fact of Andersen's existence, that he should be there at all, preceding me. This has never happened with books I first encountered as an adult. Sometimes they disappoint on rereading, but they never prove impenetrable; more often I end up exhilarated. Nor does it happen with books recommended by friends. When

I read *The Spoils of Poynton* on Steven Millhauser's recommendation, my pleasure in the book was deepened by imagining his reaction to such sentences as "Tall, straight and fair, long-limbed and strangely festooned, she stood there without a look in her eye or any perceptible intention of any sort in any other feature."

The difference stems in part from the fact that fairy tales (and not Henry James) first shaped my experience as a reader; it was in profound communion with fairy tales that my status as a reader was first negotiated. Surely my sense that these stories had their origin in me was based on this fact. When I first heard them I was very young. I had no other category at my disposal than "mine": whatever I wanted with all my heart I appropriated. To the prevailing view of the helpless reader's imagination held hostage by a piece of fiction, I opposed my own imagination's desire to possess rather than be possessed.

In other words, there was a time in my life when there was no distinction in me between reader and writer. I was, in every fiber of my being, both, simultaneously; I was becoming an artist. Nor did it hurt that Andersen's tales seemed oddly autobiographical: those breathtaking descriptions of the soul shedding her earthly plumage, strewing it mutely across an essentially shifty landscape where storks and teapots and vaporizers and snuffboxes jabbered on and on. It's no wonder I can't bear the thought of sharing whatever it was that made this possible with someone else, not even my adult self, who often seems bent on keeping the two parts separate. Andersen's tales made ideal accomplices. "'Do not come with me,' the Fairy warns the Prince, 'for with every step your longing will grow stronger . . . and if you press a kiss upon my lips, Paradise will sink deep down into the earth. . . . The sharp winds of the wilderness will whistle around you. The cold rain will drop from your hair. Sorrow and labor will be your lot.'"

These days we think we'll live forever, or at least to a hundred. And then?

You can stay by yourself in the dark wilderness of your bedroom, turning pages, all by yourself, utterly alone.

Or you can go to Paradise.

Ghost Story One

I was headed north on a train. I was going somewhere I'd been invited, an engagement for which I was to be hand-somely paid, though I was far happier to be riding on the train than to get where I was going. The sky was darkening; snow was falling. The snow was falling lightly at first but soon it was falling faster, heavier, covering the tracks. The snow was covering the tracks, piling deeper, and the brakeman told us we weren't going to be able to make it to our destination.

The man sitting in front of me objected; I'd noticed him when he got on two stops after me. He was attractive, his face with the silvery, undamageable look of a daguerreo-type, and his voice, while deep, registered not on my ears but on my frontal lobe. What on earth was there to object to? He seemed to have obtained a cocktail and was sipping it, making small, annoying sipping sounds. The tracks were impassable, the brakeman explained. He couldn't say what its name was, but this blizzard was bad enough to have one. The attractive man turned to look at me to solicit my support, the role I'm often called upon to play as a widow. It's written on you, *widow*, no matter that mourning dress has long been a thing of the past. I gave him a look back, then turned to the window.

Where were we? I could see fir trees, the lights of houses, far enough away to look like stars. We were going to have to get off the train, the conductor told us. We were somewhere between where we started and where we thought we were going. Did the place even have a name?

My husband always liked to know where he was—another way of saying he liked to know where he had been or where he was going to be. From the car he liked to call attention to the attractive white building on the university campus where his office was located and say, "I work there." Walking downtown he liked to point across the street to a spot in front of the bank and say, "That's where I catch the bus." Once, driving along the interstate, he said, "There's the exit where we landed in a Stuckey's eating pecan rolls after that tractor trailer jackknifed in front of us." It happened all the time: there would be a PBS show about the Iguazu waterfalls in Brazil and he'd say, "I've been there," as readily as he'd say the same of a seedy-looking tavern in Newark, Delaware, his purpose not to boast but to assert dominion. Unlike me, he thought of the planet, all of it, as his home.

Wherever it was we'd ended up, we gathered what luggage we had and stepped down from the first-class carriage's oppressive heat, its smell of damp upholstery and mothballs, into nostril-pinching cold, shin-deep snow, an advancing wall of wind. The brakeman had shoveled a makeshift path up an incline through frozen grass to a back road where a passenger van awaited, engine running, a heavy fellow in an orange parka behind the wheel. There were only a few of us: myself, the attractive man, a young couple in the throes of early passion, a small woman in an immense fur coat and what looked like a burqa but probably wasn't, a teenage boy in glasses. Hang on, our driver said. The roads.

The boy took the window seat behind the driver and I ended up beside him, with only the console interposing between me and the windshield. The wipers were going so fast it looked like they were going to fly away. Care for a Chiclet? the boy asked, proffering a little yellow box. When I looked surprised he informed me they'd recently been brought back into production in Mexico.

We went around a curve and the van momentarily lost traction; the small woman let out a little sound. I thought maybe I recognized her—from life, which was what this didn't seem to be. I thought maybe I knew her quite well, had known her for many years. She was sitting too far back, really, but when I craned around for a better look, the handsome man intercepted my attempt with a nod.

We'd been dislodged from the predictable, an extemporary prelude to happiness.

The van deposited us at a small inn or hotel—not a motel, since it didn't have multiple individual units and parking places. It had the outward aspect of a motel, though, a large neon sign on the office roof pointing in an unreadable direction. Oh, for God's sake, said the small woman. It looks open, the boy reassured her. Because there were no other guests, we were each given a room of our own, all the rooms commodious though not fancy. Mine was on the second floor at the end of a long hallway, the bedspread ersatz gold chintz printed with little buildings in dusty rose, possibly tearooms. There was a badly framed copy of Degas's *Absinthe Drinker* above the bed, which faced the door. Bed-facing-door was bad feng shui, I recalled my husband telling me. The bed was in "coffin position," the position facilitating removal of the corpse, feet first, though the "sitting position" of the building was unclear to me, all sides of it in this weather seeming to be private, heavy, dark. Nor did it matter which was my "lonely pillow direction." Since my husband died, all pillow directions were lonely. The room had a single window, large and with multiple lights, part of the original building no doubt, facing "five ghost direction," where I could see a snow-covered mountain.

Snow. Snow and stars. Did I want anything? That's always the question, isn't it? A drink, maybe? This place obviously had nothing like room service, but whether there was a dining room or bar remained to be seen. The room was warm, too warm, the heat similar to the heat on the train. There was a double bed. A dresser. A bookshelf filled with Reader's Digest Condensed Books. *The FBI Story, By Love Possessed. Kwaidan,* a slim volume of very short stories by a man born in Greece who moved to Japan and married a samurai's daughter. Standing at the window, I read "The Dream of Akinosuke." While he's dreaming, Akinosuke's soul emerges from his mouth in the form of a winged insect and leads him to the anthill where his wife's coffin is buried. If I wanted a drink I was going to have to leave my room to find it.

Downstairs, the desk clerk was busy with the small woman; it sounded like she was trying to make arrangements for coffee to be brought to her room in the morning even though the place had no kitchen to speak of. Louise? I said. Meanwhile the teenage boy and the attractive man were seated across the lobby on a plaid love seat, a backgammon set on the coffee table in front of them, a large rack filled with brochures on the wall behind. If we wanted, we could go tubing, visit Dracula's Castle, dine someplace called Gaslight Village. Double sixes! the boy crowed. The man was drinking a beverage similar to what he'd been drinking on the train, and when he saw me staring, he held out the bottle. Help yourself, he said.

I sat stiffly upright in a wingback chair adjacent to the love seat and took a swig, another. The whiskey was excellent, smoky and dark. How late it had become. If we'd remained on the train we'd have reached our destination by now, some luxury hotel where they'd bring you what you wanted before you'd even asked for it. The boy handed me an afghan with lots of different colored squares on a black background exactly like the one Nana made for us that someone stole from my father's room in the nursing home. We turn into thieves in our old age, the aide explained, the good ones are the worst. I could hear the dice rattle in the dice cup. I thought of Nana's face covered with powder.

You could tell, looking at a dead grandmother, that whatever had kept her alive was no longer there, just as you could tell, looking at the family dachshund, that whatever kept it alive was there in abundance. The idea of having your life drain out of you like air out of the inflatable wading pool in the backyard was terrifying. Rouged and powdered, your eyes marbles, there you would be, flat on your back. You had been somewhere and now you were nowhere, your body having assumed a semblance of mass before energy took over.

Take, the handsome man said, and the boy cursed. *Caor.* A glass bead containing ten different colors. A thunderbolt, a meteor, a round mass of flames: Papers to sign. Confusion. A finger-shaped cloud called a *craobh* used to predict the direction of the weather.

We're here for the body, the young man from the funeral parlor was saying. He was standing at the front door with his even younger helper, both with their hands clasped behind their back. The young man was the son of the man who had come to get my father's body X years earlier, except after he died my father's body had been moved to a special place in the nursing home just for bodies, so I didn't get to see it taken away. It had been midwinter then—they weren't in a big hurry. The day they came to get my husband's body was the first day of July and it was hot. Even though you couldn't see it happening, the body was starting to decompose. You could look at the smooth outward shell of the body, almost like eggshell it was so smooth, and think nothing was happening. You could look at the body and let them take it, two strangers, your husband's body. It was wearing his favorite T-shirt and khaki pants and the beautiful many-colored socks my little sister knit for him. Then it went into a refrigeration unit. He couldn't feel it.

Later I was in the restaurant at our town's one hotel, sitting with relatives around the overlarge table reserved for big parties. The table was covered with food; it was a terrible sight to see. The waitress knew me but she didn't know why I was there with all these people. Butter pats shaped like rosettes. Crumpled napkins. In the retort the temperature gets up to two thousand degrees Fahrenheit. The sound of the wind, a casting of lots, of body and bones, a silver yoke. Every night I had to rake ashes over the cinders to keep the fire alive until morning. Silver ashes and beneath them a knob of fire.

You've been asleep, the attractive man said. You were snoring, said the boy. I was asleep? I said. Only for a few moments, said the man. But then a weird thing happened. You opened your mouth and a moth came out. It hovered in front of your face for about a minute and then it flew away. What kind of a moth? I asked, and the boy laughed. I don't know what kind of moth, the man said. Aren't you wondering where it came from? Maybe there are more in there, said the boy. Don't you want to know where it went? He walked over to where the desk clerk had been sitting. I think it flew over here, the boy said. A thin stream of smoke was coming up from an ashtray the desk clerk had tried to hide behind her computer screen; there was a partly smoked cigarette in the ashtray and a little pile of ash. But what about the moth? I asked. Oh that, the man said. There was something else there all along.

Fluke

Life in the past had been filled with complication. In the past I'd have been getting the house ready and some menu would have been taking shape, the stove, the oven, the chicken, lettuces, dinnerware, flowers. Napkins. It's always been a source of amusement among people who know me how many napkins I possess. We were talking about quarantining, the danger of breaking quarantine, and my old boyfriend mentioned hearing about a place where a person who tried to run away would be severely punished. That sounds like *Brigadoon*, I said. I thought he'd have heard of *Brigadoon*, but I always forget that not everybody my age paid attention to Broadway musicals, or that even though we've known one another for years, I still don't know if he ever belonged to the Columbia Record Club. The answer to that would be something I'd have to guess at, and my guess would be he didn't. Culture, for my old boyfriend, never seemed to arrive via the usual channels. I'm sure there was a television in the house where he grew up, and that there were no prohibitions regarding its use. His mother believed that to say no to a child was tantamount to destroying the spirit of adventure.

I was living in St. Louis at the time, where it was flat and the wind wouldn't stop blowing. Spring, tornado season— the wind blew everything away except corn and soybeans. Forest Park was coming to life after a long, cold winter. "Keep your eyes peeled," I heard my father saying, waving his arms at me—but that was a forsythia bush. "Keep your eyes peeled, Kathy," said the forsythia. It was just coming into bloom. First there was one thing, a mother for instance, a father, and then there was another. And then another, a husband, a daughter, and after a while everything was different, unlike in a fairy tale where a girl is a girl, a beast a beast, pretty much from now until the end.

The sun was shining and the fountains in the Grand Basin were sparkling and I wasn't paying attention to the large dog at the other end of the leash I held in my right hand when suddenly she saw something really amazingly terrific right behind me and pulled me over backward. The fall happened so slowly I could see the tips of my feet in their black boots rising from the cement, slowly, slowly, like the feet of the Wicked Witch of the West, and I felt certain that all I had to do to keep from landing on the cement concourse would be to concentrate very hard, force my toes back down, and the next thing I knew I'd be standing upright, Lucy at my side. Instead I broke my left arm. The one I used to break the fall.

We'd ended up in different time zones, my old boyfriend and I, he on the East Coast not far from our country's first disastrous settlement, whereas I was living in the shadow of the enormous silver arch that is the gateway to the west. Each of us, that is, was living in a place where opportunity had come knocking, followed by bloodshed. I held up my arm to show him my splint. The Zoom camera made me look different from every angle, sometimes frail and perplexed, sometimes beatific, sometimes overlarge and almost masculine.

"Between today and tomorrow lies a long, long night," I said. That's what the young woman named Gertrud tells the lost adventurer in the German story *Brigadoon* is based on. Her village appears once every hundred years, sinking otherwise fathoms deep into the earth. "You will understand tomorrow what that word means," Gertrud tells the adventurer. It's a sad story, I warned my old boyfriend. Gertrud urges the adventurer not to leave the village until after the clock finishes striking twelve, thus saving him from her own grim fate but also abandoning her chance at happiness. When the adventurer once again looks for the village, he finds himself tangled in an alder thicket. Heavy drops of rain fall on his head, and an earth vapor hangs above the place like smoke.

"Alder swale," my old boyfriend corrects. He reminds me how irritable I became once, bushwhacking, when we ended up in one.

Naturally it's different in the musical. In *Brigadoon* there's no taint of mortality to the word *tomorrow*, nor is the least charnel whiff of the underworld, of things decomposing, stirred up by the dancing. In *Brigadoon*, the mist of May is in the gloaming, and the adventurer is able to reenter the village because his heart is filled with love.

When it was time, the Columbia Record Company sent me my selection. It arrived in the mailbox in a modest package, at which point I'd remove the jacket from the package and the beautiful luminous black record from the sleeve. I'd balance it carefully at its very edge between the insides of my palms as instructed by my father. I'd slip it down over the spindle until it lay flat on the turntable. It would start to spin.

This would have been 1954, the 1954 recording with Gene Kelly and Van Johnson and Cyd Charisse. "Brigadoon, Brigadoon, blooming under sable skies." I didn't know what *sable* meant back then, aside from its being a kind of fur that rich old women wore to church, the frightening old women of St. Martin-in-the-Fields, the ones who still occupy the

Pew of Judgment in my mind. The music, though—lucky for me those songs are also streaming inside me, along with the sight of a shining black record going around and around on a turntable. Even if a person didn't understand the technology, a record spinning on a turntable made sense. The needle elicited the sound. It settled into the groove, the ever-narrowing path of circumnavigation. The music was *in* there. Whatever it is a compact disc does to produce a song, you can't watch it spin. You can't lift the tone arm and blow fluff off the needle. There is no needle.

Without the material thing there is nothing to remember. There is no mystery. After I broke my arm, here is what I thought. Eric doesn't have feet.

In high school biology there had been an experiment involving a liver fluke, a pale worm the size of a grain of rice with an arrow-shaped head. You used a razor blade to bisect the head, slicing between the two "eyes"—which weren't eyes but markings, parasites having no need of eyes, especially inside a liver. After a while a new head formed on either side of the cut, and though the experiment was supposed to end there, my tenth grade self, with the steady hands of a surgeon and zero scientific aptitude, couldn't stop herself. Before the creature died it had eight heads, more than any other fluke in the class. But it didn't die because it was a freak; it died of starvation. None of the flukes lived. They could only eat liver if they thought of it as their dwelling place, it turned out.

It was difficult to tell if the flukes were alive or dead; the usual signs of life weren't apparent. We wondered whether this was why they were called flukes, until our teacher informed us *fluke* was from the Greek. For floor.

As it turns out, *fluke* doesn't only mean floor, as in flat, flat like a flounder, or the triangular plate at the tip of an anchor, one of the twin lobes of a whale's tail, but fluke can also refer to a lucky shot in billiards, a sudden gust of wind, the act of wandering, of straying, the planets. Deep underground in the ruined waterways of Hallownest the young flukefeys lie in wait, hoping to catch anything that comes by with their sharp little teeth, and as they wait they chatter, *safe, gla...little sisters...gla gla...stronger...gla gla... bigger...mother...*

During his last week I sometimes sat with Eric while he slept, petting his forehead and watching his eyeballs in motion under his shut lids. Sometimes he ground his molars; sometimes he growled and jerked his hands and feet. Sometimes he opened his eyes and looked at me and said something I couldn't understand. By this time it seemed like a word could mean anything. He was still Eric, but not-Eric as well. The times I'd felt fear before, he'd been in good health, alert and upright, angry. I kept interrupting him. I kept starting every sentence with "no." The fucking government. The fucking rain was making it impossible to get a campfire going. Our daughter was lying inside the tent, a sullen odalisque in a pale-blue sleeping bag, her honey-colored hair falling over one shoulder. So many moths flying around the propane lantern, clinging to the glass. Their bodies big, thick, like thumbs.

Other things had made me feel this way, like the 3-D horror comic that came with the glasses necessary for reading it that I bought for myself in the shadowy camp store on the boardwalk where they also sold air mattresses, tarps, lantern mantles, cigarettes, beer and wine and gin and bug repellent, though in the end it had been the smell of the comic book, that slightly pinched hollow smell damp things give off, especially wood pulp, and not the sad story it told of the misunderstood monster that broke my heart.

It was certainly a fluke that the person I chose to marry was seven years younger than me, the exact same age difference as existed between his mother and his father. When you marry someone you marry them all the way back to the beginning, past parents, grandparents, and great-grandparents, the whole ethnic pageant, all the way back to that first unspooling bolt of flesh and fat and tissue and beyond, a recognizable form receding into mere pattern and then schools of restless alien shapes shot with color, a wave, a shadow, the great shifting bottom currents.

It's different washing the body after the person has died. Running a damp washcloth over the forehead, the brow, the eyelids—the eyeballs motionless. The wish to inflict no harm is still there, elevated by the absence of response to something resembling desire. The pale-blue washcloth swimming in the pan of warm sudsy water. If emancipation has occurred, the body will not smell. The body will glow. Consciousness will have exited through the crown of the head. Meditate on the deity, incorporeal, like the reflection of the moon in water.

Signs of life. What do we even mean by that? In their mounds between Skyworld and Underworld the buried denizens of an immense former civilization have been growing restive for a very long time now. Infamous Mound 72 is filled with two layers of young women, arranged neatly in rows. Analysis of their bones, my old boyfriend told me, led archaeologists to believe the young women weren't locals. Some of them didn't have hands, some didn't have feet, though no one could say why.

Fauna

Gérard de Nerval loved animals. Did he love them more than he loved people? To look into the eyes of an animal and to be taken in by that look is the fastest way I can think of (including sex) to be transported somewhere entirely *other*, which is where Nerval spent most of his time, unlike Samuel Beckett who preferred staying inside his own head, the cows safely on the outside "chewing in enormous fields, lying and standing, in the evening silence." So many writers famously loved animals. Nabokov, like his mother, loved dachshunds. Hers were Box I and Box II; he called his dachshund Trainy "because of his being as long and as brown as a sleeping car," whereas my dachshund's name was Noodle, for reasons similarly metaphoric if not so urbane. "He has a piece of meat in his mouth," my little sister observed the day we brought him home, which is why neither one of us could ever stand to eat tongue.

Noodle was a red short-haired dachshund; I got him for my fifth birthday. Before him I'd had goldfish (Potato and Carrot) and two parakeets (Cocoa and Cupcake) but nothing warm that licked my face and squirmed in my arms and expressed urine from a small, visible penis. At some point my father observed that all my pets had been named for food. The choice of a red short-haired dachshund was based on my mother's opinion that she wouldn't need to spend time vacuuming fur; she also thought dachshunds were intelligent. My father wanted a basset hound, but they were too big and they drooled, suggesting stupidity.

Not long after I got them, the goldfish committed suicide, leaping from the bowl I'd moved to my windowsill so they could swim *en plein air*; they landed in the driveway where my father found them and provided what he said was a decent burial, though I'm sure he flushed them down the toilet. I was too young when this happened for it to traumatize me, nor had we formed a strong attachment. Cocoa died following a bath I gave him, despite having been told not to; he puffed into a furious ball of green feathers and dropped like a stone from his perch.

Owning a pet, you come face to face with death. You see the difference. The eyes like glass, like Xs. The head no longer tilted, inquisitive. The voice, silent. When you are dead you are no longer inquisitive and soon you are hard as a rock. There was the self I was then, putting the parakeet's body in the shoebox. There was the body in the shoebox. My mother said I'd get mites so we wrapped the body in an old washcloth, a pink one, the wrong color, Cocoa being a boy. My father dug a hole in the backyard at the feet of the climbing roses.

As it turned out, Noodle only lived to be two, succumbing to intervertebral disk disease, a problem common to dachshunds in which the spinal disks age faster than normal. When he died, Noodle was fourteen in dog years and his disks were even older, causing paralysis of his hind legs. Unless we choose to live with something like a box turtle or an alligator, those of us who choose to live with animals have to accept the sad fact that we're going to outlive our beloved companions—until, that is, they end up outliving us.

When I was a girl of seven, the death of my dog was the worst thing that had ever happened to me. My parents tried hushing things up but I could tell whatever was happening wasn't good. Noodle would be lying in a place that made no sense, the dining room doorway or the middle of the kitchen floor, shivering, whimpering. The smell of urine was impossible to conceal. My mother knew how this story was going to end, with the dog euthanized and the daughter inconsolable, and for this reason I understood that her distress involved me—as it so often did—and that I was not immune to what was going on. Sentimentalizing death didn't come until I connected death to myself. I had loved Noodle with all my heart, but when I looked upon the face of that which I had loved, what I saw was not the animal.

I'd given death a lot of thought. It was one of my favorite topics, in liturgy and literature. If you were good you'd go to heaven where you'd stay forever, a potentially terrifying condition, unless, like the Marsh King's daughter, you got whisked off to heaven for the mere three minutes that turned out to be so many lifetimes on earth your earthly body had dropped into dust, and all that was left of you was a withered lotus flower. My piety was theatrical. I had a blue blanket I'd drape atop my head before entering the bedroom closet, falling to my knees and closing the door behind me. I wasn't praying; I was being the Virgin Mary, getting ready to live the life that would leave everyone struck dumb with amazement. Goodness had been the goal, the goodness of a saint, but after a while it was the image of goodness I was aiming for, like being able to play *Für Elise* without ever having practiced, whereas my little sister told Mrs. Leaming, the street busybody, that the reason she never saw my father was because he was in jail.

Sainthood didn't work with Noodle and it wouldn't have worked with Mrs. Leaming. When Mrs. Leaming asked my little sister why it was she never saw my father, my sister knew foul intent when she heard it, just as she knew it would be in her own best interest to insist it was someone else who had written her name in shaky purple capital letters on the DEATHS page of the Holy Bible my Southern Baptist grandmother gave me for my seventh birthday.

Eric was three years into his cancer diagnosis—a dire prognosis that suggested he had, at most, five years to live—when we got our malamute, Lucy. I never did the math to understand what this meant for Lucy's future, given the discrepancy between dog years and ours. Eric was the dire prognosticator in our family. Not long after we met, were still filled with excessive erotic tumbling energy, he remarked as we settled into a pair of low-slung beach chairs on a wild, wind-swept beach in Nova Scotia, that the day would come when we wouldn't be able to get up out of chairs like these. As it happened, it never came to that: before the failure made itself manifest, the low-slung chairs ended up stored in the hardest to reach part of the garage behind Eric's no-longer-in-use, dearly beloved Saab convertible, the engine compartment stuffed with dryer sheets to keep out mice.

To prognosticate is to look into the future, a place, assuming it exists, I've never been all that keen on. One day my father took me into the cellar, pulled open a drawer in his workbench, and extracted a gun. He wanted me to promise that if at any time in the future he lost all his faculties, I'd put him out of his misery. The Second World War had just ended and most of the fathers on Woodale Road had a weapon concealed somewhere in the house or on proud display. My best friend Peggy's father had a Luger hidden in his handkerchief drawer under a pile of white dress hand-kerchiefs. We weren't supposed to know the gun was there but Marto told us his father had pried it from the fingers of a dead German soldier in the Ardennes Forest. Lindy's father had an unsheathed Japanese war sword hanging on the wall in his study; he'd been stationed in the Pacific but, having been a mere Signal Corpsman, he'd probably bought it on the black market. Fathers had weapons then, and handkerchief drawers. Mine neglected to mention that the gun in the workbench drawer was a starter pistol.

My lack of interest in the future is predicated on a sense of not wanting to know what's going to happen, of prefer-ring to be surprised. Following the great disappointment of imaginary numbers, I completely stopped paying atten-tion in math class, spending every class period attempt-ing to trisect an angle using a compass and straight edge, something our teacher had told us couldn't be done. The challenge of doing the impossible was what appealed to me; otherwise mathematics seemed like an exercise in fu-tility, a dreary discipline based on solving problems some-one else had already solved, not unlike the fury I felt about the mere existence of Hans Christian Andersen.

When it comes to life with a dying person it is difficult to tell the difference between the futile and the impossible. No matter how tedious the demands—organizing a com-partmented pill tray around a week's worth of thirty-four different kinds of pills totaling 420 pills in all, separated according to time of day (morning, noon, evening, bedtime), not to mention tracking down things that are vital to what's left of the dying person's happiness, that maple creemee in a wafer cone and not in a fucking dish for instance, that least favorite but crucial Nero Wolfe paperback (*Homicide Trinity*) that had to be physically applied to the upper chest totemically, like a mustard plaster, to ward off the shocking pain of shingles—that path was the one I cleaved to. "Rise up! Rise up, Eric!" I should have said that. I told myself what I was following was the path of goodness but I knew goodness wasn't going to do a bit of good.

Not long after our daughter was born, my father had a massive stroke on the right side of his brain, paralyzing the left side of his body. I returned to Philadelphia to find him in a private room in the same hospital where I'd spent two terrible weeks in the children's ward years earlier, after a tine test for tuberculosis came back positive. This had been the early fifties, and while a successful treatment for the disease had recently been developed, my parents were both traumatized, the diagnosis having been delivered with what I am certain was a degree of satisfaction by the neighborhood pediatrician. At some point my father confessed that he was afraid I was going to die like one of the consumptive heroines of the operas my mother enjoyed listening to on Saturday afternoon.

My father's faculties were, undeniably, compromised, though he could still speak and form sentences, and his memory remained intact—when I brought up that moment in the cellar with the starter pistol his blue eyes widened in horror and he lifted his good hand in a stop-right-there gesture. A week or so later he commenced narrating a series of morality tales involving a man who had lived down the street from us before I'd moved away, a man my father had always disliked on account of his tendency to showboat and to mistreat his wife. "Let the One Who Is without Sin Cast the First Stone," was the title of the first tale, alternately "Tucker Forgets and Looks Back and Turns Into a Block of Salt"—the block in homage to my horse, Peanut, for whom we'd gone out one day during my father's last visit to purchase a salt lick.

My father told me he wasn't afraid to die. Tucker was the one with all the plans up his sleeve. His poor wife, on the other hand, was a perfect candidate for Noodle Junction. They should never have gotten married in the first place. First stop, Purgatory. Second stop, Noodle Junction. When I asked, my father told me Noodle Junction was the place for people who didn't want to go to heaven. Heaven was okay if what you were after was total bliss. The story didn't have an ending, my father instructed, because it was a story about humiliation.

Before I went into the hospital I'd coveted a doll dressed in a bridal gown you could see when you looked through the heart-shaped cellophane opening in the lid of the box she came in. This was before Barbie; the doll was smaller but also, like Barbie, blond, with pixie features, a face about as much not like mine as a face could be. I forget who it was who brought me the doll. I don't think it was either of my parents; it might have been a neighbor. I received quite a lot of presents during my hospital stay, including a weird succulent in a bird-shaped planter and a beautiful illustrated edition of *The Adventures of Robin Hood*. If a present came wrapped, I removed the wrapping paper, but that was where my engagement with the present ended. The doll stayed in her box: I never undid the little wires attaching her to the cardboard at the wrists and ankles. Neither of my parents explained why I needed to be sent to the hospital, only that I was going in for "tests." Of course like any high-strung girl born into a repressed fifties household, I was adept at reading clues. The sighs. The exchanged looks. The dish of fruit Jell-O swiftly deposited on my hospital bed tray followed by the hasty retreat. My mother would stand up. My father would stand up. He could do that then.

Ghost Story Two

The driver let me out at the foot of an unpaved lane bordered by trees, their crowns black and still as stone. He wasn't supposed to go further, he said, giving me the once-over. My husband had died a year earlier and I was used to being examined for symptoms, as if widowhood might be catching. The young lady took care of it, the driver said, when I reached for my purse. Then he drove away.

Flickering lights in the distance or near at hand, it was impossible to say—they could have been bugs, windows, stars. I kept walking without knowing where I was going, losing my footing from time to time on a root or a rock. It was very dark; it was the dark of the moon. Eventually I arrived at what seemed to be a back entrance; the cottage was set on a rocky promontory overlooking a large body of water. I could tell the water was there even though I couldn't see it from where I stood, the way you sense a person in the next room even if you think the room is empty. The water would be too cold for swimming and, being glacial, so deep you could never get to the bottom of it.

"Hello?" I called. "Hello?" The screen door opened into a large kitchen where the refrigerator was running noisily and a faucet was dripping. When I looked for a light switch I found an external junction box with a monkey-face adapter that gave me a small shock when I hit the button. I saw a bowl and a spoon. A cutting board and knife. There was a lot of sound in the room, considering the fact that this was the middle of nowhere. The refrigerator, the faucet, tree frogs, crickets, the lake. Summer was ending and fall was coming. The casement windows were open wide. Somewhere school would be starting soon.

I saw an ancient cookstove and a brand-new microwave, price tag attached, a sleeve of saltines inside. The refrigerator was empty, the ice cube trays full. A very good toleware tray hung above the door into the living room, similar to the ones painted by old Mrs. Prevett, whose granddaughter my best friend Peggy and I used to enjoy tormenting when we were girls. When we told Lindy tomato juice was blood, she believed us. It was too easy to˙ be fun, really.

The floor needed sweeping. Someone had tracked in dirt and pine needles, and there were mouse droppings under the worktable—I saw this even before I saw the note. When I opened what looked like a broom closet it turned out to be a pantry empty of everything except a metal flour canister and a set of hand-painted bowls like the one on the worktable, the same as the bowls my father stole from the shop where my mother worked, because the owner was too cheap to pay her a decent salary. That dame has more money than you can shake a stick at, my father said. Not to mention those cocker spaniels. Out of the corner of my eye I saw a mouse scamper across the pantry floor and disappear through the arched entry to its house, exactly like a mouse in a cartoon.

It was late. It had been a long time since I'd seen my daughter. I tried to remember when that had been. Maybe the last time I saw her was when the visiting nurse sent her into the kitchen for the morphine. It was in a little glass bottle with a calibrated dropper, on the same shelf in the refrigerator as the homemade peach jam and the tomato chutney. I washed and dried the bowl and spoon; the inside of the bowl had a picture in it of a blue horse reared up on its hind legs. The other bowls in the set included a cow, a pig, and a farmer, but the only desirable bowl was the one showing the horse, my daughter's favorite. The spoon I'd never seen before.

Hi Mom, said the note. Sweet dreams.

Really, I was here because of the outdoor shower. Of all the things my husband had wanted with a strong and unbendable passion, an outdoor shower would have to have been near the top of the list, after the wholesale acceptance by economists of the second law of thermodynamics, and the annihilation of Donald Trump. We prepared in a weak and bendable way to find a place to install such a shower, settling on the side of the garage facing away from the road, a location that also turned out to face the part of our neighbors' yard on the other side of the lilac hedge where they planned to erect an immense red play structure on which their little children, swinging, would get a great view of my husband's naked body.

His body. There had been the heft and substance of it. I could look at the outside of his body and have no idea about the terrible things going on inside. I could look at my own arm in the same spirit; if it weren't for the glove of skin it would be a terrible sight to see. My husband's body had heft and substance when we met; he had worked summers as a bricklayer to help pay for his college education. As time wore on we all got older, but my husband's body remained strong. People thought I was exaggerating the seriousness of his illness, partly because of the way he looked, and partly because fiction writers are known to make things up. The skin held the parts together. Then the corruption set in and the unity of the body was forever destroyed.

There were four beds in the cottage. Three of them were upstairs, but the fourth, the best, was at the far end of the screen porch overlooking the lake. I was tired, yes, and no one could blame me, for the hour was late. This wasn't a bedroom so there was no bedside table, but I found a flashlight on the windowsill beside a Golden Book I thought I recognized, and tucked under it the spiral notebook Lucy tried to eat when she was a puppy. Dr. E [chewed] Roxan [chewed] Send CD R [chewed] CAT scan [chewed] everything f [chewed] Andriole's offi [chewed] kidney docs [chewed] follow up xra [chewed] obturator nerve [chewed] of car nerve [chewed] PSA undetectable .02 0.03 0.1 [chewed] super sensitive det [end of page one].

I slipped between the sheets, taking care not to wake my daughter. She was lying there in the exact middle of the bed, so small in her flannel Bonne Nuit nightgown, the one that made her cry when it went in the wash. The sheets were white like the sheets ghosts wear. There had been a ghost in my past. His name was John Waite and he lived for a while with me and the first husband in the white farmhouse atop a hill in the town of Woodbury. The dogs wouldn't go into the room where John stood looking out the window—not in a sheet but a pillar of light you saw without your eyes the same way I'd heard the lake without my ears. He was a sad ghost, Earlene Leonard, the town historian, told me. John Waite's young wife died in childbirth and he felt like it was his fault. Sex, Earlene elaborated darkly. I'd been told Earlene was an "old maid," which back then was what the old-timers called lesbians. She had been a star baseball player when she was a girl—what I had longed to be in my romantic heart of hearts, which is why despite my total lack of talent I used all the money I earned selling hideous greeting cards to people like Mrs. Trimble to buy a Louisville Slugger bat. I tried babysitting, too, for a Quaker family with five children and a goat and two dogs and two cats and some guinea pigs and gerbils that all ran loose around the house. Dinner's in the fridge, the mother's note had said, but when I looked all I could find was a block of cheese and some condiments.

Before I knew what was going on, sometimes when I walked past the door into what had once been the living room of the white farmhouse, I used to think I saw a man in the far corner. He was just past middle age, balding, hunched over. For a while he spoke to me and my young friend Chris via a Ouija board. "Are there other ghosts here besides you?" "I permit no others." "If you can come in anytime, why must we let you in?" "You're filled with doors."

"To think is to mark the closed threshold of one's own consciousness." J. M. Coetzee said this about Samuel Beckett's inability to fathom the whale's "great, scheming animal brain." And it is true, you can only be haunted if you believe in an Other. The pages of the Golden Book still had my husband's scent, the one he acquired during his final year when he took, mysteriously, to using a cologne stick. "Once upon a time," I read, "there was a funny dog named Crispin's Crispian. He was named Crispin's Crispian . . ." My daughter opened her eyes and stared up at me. I could tell she wasn't awake. "Because he belonged to himself," she said. Then she closed her eyes and rolled over.

Eventually I fell into an uneasy sleep, the kind where you remain unsure about whether you're asleep or not. For example, the moon had been an all but invisible crescent when I arrived at the cottage. Even given the overhanging boughs of the trees, I knew it was the absence of moonlight that made it difficult for me to see where I was going. When I woke, though, the moon was full and overlarge, like one of those so-called supermoons, only this moon was more super, as if it had exceeded perigee and was coming closer to Earth than it was supposed to. It wasn't frightening. One year for Christmas I'd asked for a telescope, and what I got when I looked through it was an out of focus view of the moon and nothing more, wobbly like pudding.

I could see the supermoon's individual craters beyond the screen window, how deep they were, the Sea of Tranquility, bigger and sparkling, bright black and shot with sparkles, the night sky, the lake. "Look," I said to my daughter, but then I saw her side of the bed was empty.

What was wrong with me, I wondered, that I couldn't make the people in bed with me stay there.

There was a hook and eye latch on the porch door which swung open over what looked like empty space, beneath which a long set of ladderlike steps led to a narrow footbridge.

The bridge was made of something like burlap, thick burlap, and there was a guardrail, but only on the right side for some reason. Down below was a vast body of water, the surface broken at intervals by whitecaps, so far below as to be like lashes, white lashes against the colorless face of the water. The horizon? Not even visible. This was no lake!

The minute I set foot on the bridge it began to sway. I continued for a short distance. There was no way on earth I could make it to the other side, if such a thing existed. I took another step and felt the bridge swing to the right, tipping me to the left, handrail-less side. I should turn around and go back, I knew, though turning would be awkward. Besides which, there was someone behind me. "We have to turn around," I said. "Now!" I couldn't look back to see him but I knew it was Eric. He was in the wheelchair we'd borrowed for him to use during his last month, when his legs didn't have the will left in them to hold him aloft. Of course he couldn't turn around or back up. We would have to stay there like that.

I could picture him, his beautiful face swollen by steroids. I wondered if he could picture me, balanced there, facing nothing.

Bagatelles

In the sixty-fourth year of her life, having fought cancer and—if not having utterly vanquished it, at least having brought it to its knees—my friend Lois bought herself a very expensive piano, a Bösendorfer.

Bösendorfer pianos are made in Vienna. They are known to produce a darker, richer sound than other pianos; the keys, when depressed, hold the tone longer and the bass notes are more powerful. It takes five years (including the time to dry the wood) to produce a Bösendorfer; the company calls itself "the world's slowest piano builder."

In the thirty-first year of his life, Gustave Flaubert, who famously took three days to write a simple transition that took him as many weeks to perfect, wrote, "And yet I feel that I must not die before the style that I have in my head has been able to sound somewhere, over the din of parrots and crickets." He complained that there wasn't room to say what needed to be said to make his lovers get off their horses, have intercourse, and continue with their lives. It all had to be "very fast and incidental, to be as if thrown away, almost unnoticeable."

It is four in the afternoon in Seattle. Lois's dog, Lily, is walking in circles the way dogs do when they're preparing to lie down, flattening the invisible grass that grows out of hardwood floors. Lois is playing Beethoven's Opus 126 for me, a series of six bagatelles, the last music for piano he wrote before he died. During this same period he was composing his astonishing late string quartets, the quartets and the bagatelles having in common a tendency to juxtapose the sublime and the antic, the music appearing to make a mysterious and often all but inaudible transit from one mode to the other, as mysterious as the shift from pain to its absence in the composer's final years. On the face of it the contrasts are so wild you'd think the overall effect would be unconsonant, chaotic even, yet—as Lois plays it for me—the music seems to inhabit both realms equally, almost as if simultaneously, the sweetness made more sweet by its leap into disharmony, the disharmony more jarring for its embrace of sweetness. "Beethoven's art (and perhaps his life) can be viewed as the outcome of opposing drives toward integration and dissociation," in one critic's words. "Repellent, if not unintelligible," in the words of another.

A transition—the moment of transition—when achieved as perfectly as Beethoven did in his bagatelles and the late quartets, is able to perform this sleight of hand, the moment-between, the ghost-moment, inhabited by both parts. According to Lois, this kind of ghost-moment is facilitated by the instrument, since the sound produced when you depress a piano key—even without the use of the sustaining pedal—persists well beyond the moment the key is depressed.

The six bagatelles comprising Opus 126 were published in 1825, two years prior to Beethoven's death. By the time of their composition, his deafness—the first symptoms of which had appeared before he reached the age of thirty— was all but total. Beethoven claimed he lost his hearing in a fit of temper, that he fell over and stood up deaf. He also claimed he went deaf from repeatedly immersing his head in a bucket of cold water to stay awake. His ears were his greatest gift from his creator, "the great Tonemaster above." To Beethoven, the loss of hearing was shameful, tantamount to a sin. In a letter to a friend he referred to his deafness as "the demon that has set up habitation in my ears." He considered suicide but rejected the idea in the famous Heiligenstadt Testament, written for his brothers in 1802. "It is said that I must now choose patience for my guide . . . until it please the inexorable Parcae to break the thread."

Patience was never Beethoven's long suit, nor did he suffer fools gladly, and the older and deafer he became, the fewer the fools he'd suffer, gladly or not. Meanwhile he maintained a watchful relationship with the Fates, eyes on the scissors. He was fifty-five years old when he composed Opus 126. He wasn't on his deathbed but he was dying, his physical system, always a losing proposition (diabetes? lead poisoning? cirrhosis of the liver? renal necrosis? pancreatitis? portal hypertension? syphilis? hepatitis? Whipple's disease? sarcoidosis?) rehearsing its final breakdown. Wild and unkempt, waving his arms around and around and with cotton wool sticking out of his ears, he was rumored on one occasion to have caused a stampede of cattle. When Luigi Cherubini ran into him on the street he referred to him as an "unlicked bear cub." People listened to the *Grosse Fuge* and thought he'd taken leave of his senses. "We know there is something there but we don't know what it is," they said.

"Art demands of us that we do not stand still," Beethoven said in reply.

The world, as seen, is experienced for the most part like an unbroken bolt of fabric. What your eyes see is one comprehensive thing unreeling before them, and any appearances or disappearances are part of that one unreeling thing. A man enters your field of vision from the right and exits to the left—it's all still your single field of vision, even if the man parachutes in from above. Whereas the world, as heard, is always experienced for the most part discontinuously. Of course there are some constants, the sound of your breathing, for example, so low-pitched as to seem inaudible. But the things your ears hear—a person speaking, wind in the trees, a barking dog, the chaotic opening measures of the sixth bagatelle—tend to occur intermittently.

Hearing. It's a mystery, really, what music *is*. Signs on paper transliterated into sounds that travel through the air to enter a human body via the ears but also through the skin, the bones, the brain. Listening to music can help a stroke victim overcome left-sidedness. Listening to music can help people with Parkinson's disease walk. Music may enter through our ears. But what is it that is entering? What was Beethoven hearing when he composed the bagatelles? Was this a memory of sound, a replication of auditory memory, a memory of the essentially fitful experience of hearing? "My dominion is not easily reached!" Beethoven said. "I must accustom myself to think out at once the whole, as soon as it shows itself, with all the voices, in my head."

During the course of his life Beethoven composed twenty-four bagatelles; he referred to them as *Kleinigkeiten*, or "small things." Opus 126, though, is anything but small. In its complexity, the variousness of its parts, its returns and departures, but most especially in its great, strange moments of transition, the sense Beethoven provides is that of a space, the small space the cycle occupies that is able to contain all of space itself. You might say the bagatelles comprising Opus 126 contain within them the universe that is the amazing Quartet in B-flat. You might say that the smaller the container, the greater the possibility of perfection. This is the "fast and incidental, almost unnoticeable" spirit in which Flaubert said his lovers had to get down off their horses.

Many years have elapsed since Lois first played the six bagatelles for me, not long after she bought the Bösendorfer. Opus 126 is a piece of music she has strong feelings about, about the way it ought to be played, just as she has strong feelings about the piano itself. Lois hated her former piano, a Steinway, the entire time it was in her possession. Nor would she recommend any recordings of the piece. None of them were right, she insisted. If I wanted to replicate the experience of hearing Opus 126, I'd just have to come back to Seattle.

When Eric and I talked about his memorial service, he was full of ideas. I knew, for starters, that he wanted to have one. Ever since the cancer diagnosis he'd liked the idea of a large group of people singing "Wake up, wake up, you sleepyhead," even though that would have required him to be present in a casket at something more like a funeral, which wasn't what he had in mind. In the end a few possibilities rose to the top of his list. He wanted Louise to read a poem; he wanted Lois to play the piano.

A very long time ago we used to have a regular date with two other couples—Lois and Deb, Mark and Wally—at the

Dugout, a hole-in-the-wall restaurant on the road leading from Barre to the granite quarries. The waitstaff, quaintly, had configured our pairings heterosexually. Back then the lines of friendship ran deep; over the years Eric's and my friendship with Deb and Lois only deepened. Lois had trained as a concert pianist at Oberlin, but somewhere along the line she decided performing in public was a torture she didn't really ever want to have to endure. "Of course she'll do it," Eric said, speaking with the authority of a friend and not a dying person.

I can't replicate the sound of what we heard that day in College Hall. Visual images can be replicated in language, a sound—especially the sound of a piece of music—cannot. Virginia Woolf describes the scene Mrs. Ramsay sees out the window as a "great plateful of blue water . . . the hoary lighthouse, distant, austere," and you're able to see what Mrs. Ramsay is seeing, whereas—aside from human voices—Virginia Woolf has always pretty much avoided describing sound. It seems possible Eric—earless in whatever bardo he may have been occupying then—may be better suited to that task.

In Tibetan Buddhism, the soul is guided along the forty-nine-day journey into the afterlife by the Great Liberation Through Hearing. The eyes have closed forever, the temporal realm no longer available. The body is lying on its right side in the lion posture, the same one the Buddha assumed when he was dying. I like to think of Beethoven lying in this position. The story has him lying there while a storm is in process outside; at the very moment he raises his fist to the heavens to curse the gods there's a loud clap of thunder, after which he dies.

I know, though, that the story about Beethoven lifting his clenched fist to curse the gods fails to take into account the fact that a dying person will lift an arm or arms immediately before death for no apparent reason other than to open the airways, to expand the rib cage—just before expelling the final breath. My father's nurse told me this when I was keeping vigil at his deathbed.

My father's eyes had been closed for hours and he hadn't uttered a sound. His ears, though—his ears remained open, mysterious conduits to consciousness. At some point I started singing "Take Me Out to the Ball Game" to him, the same song he used to sing to me as a lullaby, and when I got to "I don't care if I never get back" my father sang along.

"What seems to me the highest and most difficult achievement of art is not to make us laugh or cry, not to arouse our lust or rage, but to do what nature does—to set us dreaming," said Gustave Flaubert.

"Now they were so close to the horses they could hear them munching leaves."

Aurélia

When I was a pretentious girl of sixteen, with a prancing in-tellect and an overweening desire for Romance, I sailed to Europe on the student ship *Aurelia*. To cross an ocean is of course a form of transition, a *crossing*, in this case from Woodale Road, locus of all things American and childish, to Europe, birthplace of the most interesting forms of sin. Blaz-ing blue, blazing white, sky and sea and smokestack—that's what I recollect about the voyage, as well as having to sleep in a cabin crammed with four bunk beds and eight hormonally charged young women on a ship teeming with potential ro-mantic partners of every stripe everywhere you looked.

Here's what I didn't want: someone my own age who thought beer-drinking games were fun. These would be "boys."

Here's what I wanted: someone older, preferably someone who would ferry me away to Alexandria, "winepress of love." I affected a paisley scarf, peasant style, huge dark glasses, a Russian accent, a limited understanding of English; I said my name was Lubimya (one of the few Russian words I knew, meaning "love"). In addition to high school students headed to Europe for the summer, and college students headed to Europe for a semester, there were college teachers on the ship getting paid to run workshops. There was a bald man teaching a drawing class who found me exotic, and when he asked me to pose for his class, I feigned misunderstanding. Here's what I didn't want: an old bald man who had fallen for my disguise.

At some point I entered the ship theater, where *The Seventh Seal* was playing. I slid into a back row seat late; I had no idea what was happening on the screen, a man in a black cloak with a round white face speaking a foreign language. I was on a boat to Europe that contained a movie theater! I had never seen anything like this in my life. On my right: a handsome college student, outlier of his group, headed to Denmark for his junior year abroad. I dropped the Russian accent but retained the dark glasses which were prescription and hid the fact that I needed regular glasses. The student was a philosophy major at Oberlin, a copy of *Either/Or* prominent on his lap, and for a time I became obsessed with Kierkegaard. My usual mistake, confusing scholarship and romance, though I have to admit I learned a lot this way.

Romantic obsession taken to the point of madness is the subject—maybe more specifically the landscape—of Gérard de Nerval's novella *Aurélia*, written not long after the author was released from the sanatorium in Passy. My romantic obsession with the handsome college student didn't take me to the point of madness but merely across the Atlantic Ocean, whereas Nerval's love for Jenny Colon— the fetching blond cantatrice from Boulogne who is said to have been the real Aurélia—remained unrequited; it took him all the way to that final transition from this world to the next. "I was in a deserted place, a steep rocky slope in the middle of the woods. A single house, which I thought I recognized, overlooked this desolate landscape. I kept losing my way in the maze. Tired of fighting my way through the rocks and brambles, now and then I would seek out an easier path along the wooded trails. They're waiting for me over there! I thought to myself."

Aurelia, Aurélia. There's a kind of transit that occurs between the place in your mind where memory resides, as firmly planted as the house you grew up in, and the operative tool of thought, designed to transport you and your memory elsewhere, as if across the ocean on a boat. The ship kept appearing at first on the horizon, an abstraction like the *Kahana*, but then close up, particular, a vision of the particular self at a particular moment, requisite to memory's need for a host to carry it as far away from memory lane as possible. The excitement of having been—of *being*—that girl in the paisley scarf, waiting with almost impossible avidity for something, anything, to happen, broke the wall between memory and thought. The psyche went into spasms of anticipation. A mysterious transaction was about to take place: something rote was about to become something alive. This is how the associative moment occurs.

The *Aurelia* I traveled to Europe on flew an American flag but (like my long-ago self) had assumed a variety of nationalities and names. Originally christened the *Huascaran*, for a Peruvian mountain, it had been built in Hamburg in 1938 as a repair vessel for Nazi warships, the original inspection conducted by Hermann Göring. *Aurelia* is the Latin translation of the Greek work for chrysalis, the gold-colored pupa of the butterfly, emblem of metamorphosis and hiddenness. In 1947 the *Huascaran* became the *Beaverbrae,* a postwar immigrant liner. By 1951 it had made fifty-two trips and transported 33,255 displaced persons from Germany to Canada. In 1955 it was sold to an Italian line and was totally overhauled, provided with air-conditioning and a lido pool. It made its maiden voyage as the *Aurelia* in 1955, but it wasn't until the summer of 1960 that the U.S. Council on Student Travel chartered it and filled it with young people. Eventually it became the *Romanza,* a standard cruise ship, and at last the *Romantica,* catching fire and burning out of control sixty miles off the Cypriot city of Limassol on October 4, 1997, before getting towed to Alexandria to be broken up into parts.

To Alexandria! Winepress of love, graveyard of ships. "As if long prepared for this, as if courageous, / bid her farewell, the Alexandria that is leaving," wrote Cavafy. "Above all do not be fooled, do not tell yourself / it was only a dream . . ." "Dream is a second life," the narrator of *Aurélia* tells us. "I have never been able to cross through those gates of ivory or horn which separate us from the invisible world without a sense of dread."

~

In the last month of my husband's life he became preoccupied with the gold ring he had been wearing until it no longer fit over his swollen knuckle. The ring had belonged to my uncle Fred and came to me upon my uncle's death—at some point my husband decided he liked it and wanted to wear it. The ring is heavy with a rectangular "face" in which the initials F. D. (for Fred Davis) appear, the D larger than the F due to a triangular space above the F where a diamond has been set. I never thought the ring was especially attractive (it isn't), but my husband wore it as religiously as his wedding ring. He was specific about not wanting to see it cremated along with his mortal remains and the Rex Stout novel he hadn't quite finished reading.

During the final month of his life, my husband had a lot to say about the ring. "There should be a storm drain in the room," he told me and our daughter. The water, which was the essence of the three of us, was going to be rising, our emotions lapping at our ankles, up to our knees and thighs. He wanted us to know that while there was no way to stop the water from rising, as long as he was wearing the ring it would act as a drain. My husband wasn't hallucinating; he was coherent and conversational. He provided this information as breezily as you might remind someone that tomorrow night they should cover the basil plants. He also pointed out that the ring had a hairline crack in it at the base of the shank; if he was going to be able to wear it, it needed to be repaired and resized. But he also said, "Suppose the ring is the drain of my bardo. Then fixing it stoppers up the drain. Do I want that to happen sooner or later?"

"Chance does strange things," the narrator of *Aurélia* tells us; he has only recently learned of his beloved's death. He remembers a ring he gave her, an "antique ring set with an opal carved in the shape of a heart," and because the ring was too large for her finger he decided to have it cut down in size, only realizing his mistake when he heard the sound of a saw and could see blood flowing. In the dreamscape of *Aurélia*, most material objects end by seeming, like Aurélia herself, evanescent, elusive. But the ring, because it isn't a dream ring, acquires heft, as does a second ring, silver, slipped off the narrator's finger in Notre-Dame-de-Lorette while he piously kneels at the altar of the Virgin, and a third ring he wears shortly thereafter to the osteological exhibits at the Museum of Natural History. When rings are received or bestowed as gifts, they have a negative association for Nerval, the opposite, when perceived as *ordalia*, as in the case of the third ring, likewise silver.

Eventually the narrator leaves the museum and goes out into the garden, where it's pouring rain. What a shame! he thinks. All the women and children are going to get drenched. Then he realizes things are far more serious. This is the beginning of the real Flood!, he thinks. "The water was rising in the nearby streets; I ran down the rue Saint-Victor and, believing I might be able to stem the global tide, I threw the ring I had bought at Saint-Eustache into the deepest part of the water. It was roughly at this moment that the rain tapered off and a ray of sun burst forth."

On the *Aurelia*, I spent a lot of time standing alone at the rail, smoking; I thought this was a good look for me, the swells of the North Atlantic surging dark and impenetrable in all directions. The ship's forward movement made it impossible to comprehend the nature of the tidal motion going on below "like the vessels or veins that wind through the lobes of the brain," as Nerval describes it, "streams . . . made up of living beings in a molecular state, which only the speed at which I was traveling made it impossible to distinguish." The ship was so small, the size of a flea—the size of an atom of a flea—by comparison with the enormous ball that was the earth, never mind the entire universe. "That's all you get," my husband cautioned on his deathbed. "The ripple is what we live on, and we get to pull up one ripple of the water the way cars create a vacuum as they race around a track like clamshells. That's all you get, a ripple, a little bitty thing, a wave, because the world is so huge, you just get to use it for a little while."

When I was a sixteen-year-old girl riding the *Aurelia* to Europe, my husband was a nine-year-old boy with fifty-seven years left in which to do all the things he ended up doing in his life. The course of the transit is impossible to fathom, except via the remarkable apparatus of association. Even the North Atlantic has its limits. From Pier 84 in New York City to the great port of Le Havre. Whatever I was pretending to be that week on the ship is exactly what I was, the implausible outward trappings of the infinitely smaller thing inside.

Portions of this memoir were originally published, in slightly different form, as "Time Passes," in *Grist*; "Lost," in *Salmagundi*; "Why I Don't Like Reading Fairy Tales," in *Mirror, Mirror on the Wall*; "Bagatelles," in the *Review of Contemporary Fiction*; and "Maple Dresser," in *Political Objects*.

I want to thank Jin Auh and Alex Andriesse, for their inspired reading and advice.

Kathryn Davis is the author of eight novels, the most recent of which is *The Silk Road*. She has received the Kafka Prize for fiction by an American woman; both the Morton Dauwen Zabel Award and the Katherine Anne Porter Award from the American Academy of Arts and Letters; a Guggenheim Fellowship; and the Lannan Foundation Literary Award. She teaches at Washington University in St. Louis and lives in Vermont.

The text of *Aurelia, Aurélia* is set in Arno Pro.
Book design by Rachel Holscher.
Composition by Bookmobile Design & Digital
Publisher Services, Minneapolis, Minnesota.
Manufactured by McNaughton & Gunn on acid-free,
100 percent postconsumer wastepaper.